# Garden Plants
## *for*
# Atlantic Canada

*Duncan Kelbaugh* • *Alison Beck*

LONE
PINE

Lone Pine Publishing

**The Publisher: Lone Pine Publishing**
10145 – 81 Avenue
Edmonton, AB, T6E 1W9 Canada
Website: www.lonepinepublishing.com

**Library and Archives Canada Cataloguing in Publication**

Kelbaugh, Duncan, 1953-
      Best garden plants for Atlantic Canada / Duncan Kelbaugh, Alison Beck.

Includes index.
ISBN-13: 978-1-55105-578-7
ISBN-10: 1-55105-578-3.--

      1. Plants, Ornamental--Atlantic Provinces.  2. Gardening--Atlantic Provinces.  I. Beck, Alison, 1971-  II. Title.

SB453.3.C2K438 2007          635.9'09715          C2006-905715-X

Front cover photographs by Tamara Eder except where noted (clockwise from top right): John Davis rose (Robert Ritchie), iris, lilac, daylily, sweet potato vine, daylily (Tim Matheson), lily (Laura Peters), columbine, crabapple (Tim Matheson), lily (Erika Flatt).

All photos by Tamara Eder, Tim Matheson and Laura Peters except:
Joan de Grey 141b; Therese D'Monte 144b; Don Doucette 108b; Jen Fafard 138a; Derek Fell 47b, 139a, 143a, 144a, 165; Erika Flatt 95a, 109b, 134b, 142a, 166b; Jennie Fougere 10a; Saxon Holt 139b; Duncan Kelbaugh 1, 4, 134a; Liz Klose 118a, 169a&b; Dawn Loewen 8b&c; Janet Loughrey 52b, 128b, 143b; Marilynn McAra 138b, 140b, 141a; Kim O'Leary 12a, 133a, 136a, 153b; Allison Penko 10b, 20b, 47a, 60a, 76a, 85a, 86b, 92a, 94b, 96b, 101, 103a, 104a&b, 127b, 133b, 137a, 159a, 161, 162a, 163a, 164b, 168a; Photos.com 140a, 145a; Robert Ritchie 48a, 53b, 112a, 117a&b, 119a&b, 120a, 121a, 123a&b, 129a, 153a; Elizabeth Schleicher 115a&b; Leila Sidi 145b; Joy Spurr 124a; Peter Thompstone 28a, 54a, 57a, 65a&b, 79a; Mark Turner 52a; Don Williamson 131b, 135a&b, 148a; Tim Wood 87b.

This book is not intended as a 'how-to' guide for eating garden plants. No plant or plant extract should be consumed unless you are certain of its identity and toxicity and of your potential for allergic reactions.

We acknowledge the financial support of the Government of Canada through the Book Publishing Industry Development Program (BPIDP) for our publishing activities.

PC: *P13*

# Table of Contents

# Introduction

Starting a garden can seem like a daunting task, but it is also an exciting and rewarding adventure. With so many plants to choose from, the challenge is deciding which ones and how many to include in your garden. This book is intended to give beginning gardeners the information they need to start planning and planting gardens of their own. It provides a wide variety of plant descriptions, cultural information and tips to get you on your way to producing a beautiful and functional landscape.

The summer growing season in Atlantic Canada is quite short. The winters, though cold, ensure a good period of dormancy and plenty of flowers in spring. Annual rainfall is plentiful, but winter rains that remove the protective snow cover can be hard on some plants. The soil, though rocky along the coast and in the highlands, supports a variety of healthy plants.

Hardiness zones and frost dates are two terms often used when discussing climate and gardening. The Canadian Hardiness zones are based on the minimum possible winter temperatures and other factors that influence plant survival such as rainfall and snow cover. Plants are rated based on the zones in which they grow successfully. The last frost date in spring combined with the first frost date in fall allows us to predict the length of the growing season and gives us an idea of when we can begin planting out in spring.

Microclimates are small areas that are generally warmer or colder than the surrounding area. Buildings, fences, trees and other large structures can provide extra shelter in winter but may trap heat in summer, thus creating a warmer microclimate. The bottoms of hills are usually colder than the tops but may not be as windy. Take advantage of these areas when you plan your garden and choose your plants; you may even grow out-of-zone plants successfully in a warm, sheltered location.

## Getting Started

When planning your garden, start with a quick analysis of the garden as it is now. Plants have different requirements, and it is best to put the right plant in the right place rather than to try and change your garden to suit the plants you want.

Knowing which parts of your garden receive the most and least amounts of sunlight will help you choose the proper plants and decide where to plant them. Light is classified into four basic groups: full sun (direct, unobstructed light all or most of the day); partial shade or partial sun (direct sun for about half the day and shade for the rest); light shade (shade all or most of the day with some sun filtering through to ground level); and full shade (no direct sunlight). Most plants prefer at least some direct sun, but many can adapt to a range of light levels.

The soil is the foundation of a good garden. Plants not only use the soil to hold themselves upright, but also rely on the many resources it holds: air, water, nutrients, organic matter and a host of microbes. The particle size of the soil influences the amount of air, water and nutrients it can hold. Sand, with the largest particles, has lots of air space and allows water and nutrients to drain quickly. Clay, with the smallest particles, is high in nutrients but has very little air space. Water is therefore slow to penetrate clay and slow to drain from it.

Soil acidity or alkalinity (measured on the pH scale) influences the amount and type of nutrients available to plants. A pH of 7 is neutral; a lower pH is more acidic. Most plants prefer soil with a pH of 5.5–7.5. Soil testing kits are available at most garden centres, and soil samples can be sent to testing facilities for a more thorough analysis. This will give you an idea of what plants will do well in your soil and what amendments might need to be made to your soil.

## Hardiness Zones Map

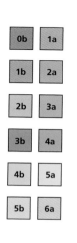

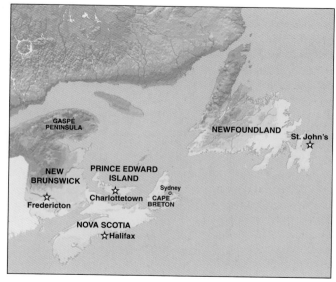

Compost is one of the best and most important amendments you can add to any type of soil. Compost improves soil by adding organic matter and nutrients, introducing soil microbes, increasing water retention and improving drainage. Compost can be purchased, or you can make it in your own backyard.

## Selecting Plants

It's important to purchase healthy plants that are free of pests and diseases. Such plants will establish quickly in your garden and won't introduce problems that may spread to other plants. You should have a good idea of what the plant is supposed to look like at maturity—the colour and shape of the leaves and the habit of the plant—and then inspect the plant for signs of disease or insect damage.

Many plants are container grown. This is an efficient way for nurseries and greenhouses to grow plants, but when plants grow in a restricted space for too long, they can become pot bound, with their roots densely encircling the inside of the pot. Avoid purchasing plants in this condition; they are often stressed and can take longer to establish. It is often possible to remove pots temporarily to look at the condition of the roots. You can check for soil-borne insects, rotten roots and girdling or pot-bound roots at the same time. Roots wrapping densely around the inside of a pot must be lightly pruned or teased apart before planting.

## Planting Basics

The following tips apply to all plants.

• Prepare the garden before planting. Remove weeds, make any needed amendments and dig or till the soil in preparation for planting if you are starting a new landscape. This may be more difficult in established beds to which you want to add a single plant. The prepared area should be the size of the plant's mature root system.

• Settle the soil with water. Good contact between the roots and the soil is important, but if you press the soil down too firmly, as often happens when you step on the soil, you can cause compaction, which reduces the movement of water through the soil and leaves very few air spaces. Instead, pour water in as you fill the hole with soil. The water will settle the soil evenly without allowing it to compact.

• Unwrap the roots. It is always best to remove any container before planting to give roots the chance to spread out naturally when planted. In particular, you should remove plastic containers, fibre pots, wire and burlap before planting trees. Fibre pots decompose very slowly, if at all, and draw moisture away from the plant. Burlap may be synthetic, which won't decompose, and wire can eventually strangle the roots as they mature. The only exceptions to this rule are the peat pots and pellets used to start annuals and vegetables; these

Gently remove container.

Ensure proper planting depth.

Backfill with soil.

decompose and can be planted with the young transplants. Even peat pots should be sliced down the sides and any of the pot that will be exposed above ground removed to prevent water from being drawn away from the roots.

• Accommodate the rootball. If you prepared your planting spot ahead of time so it will accommodate the mature roots, your planting hole will only need to be big enough to accommodate the root ball with the roots spread out slightly. Otherwise, you will have to prepare a space at least twice the size of the rootball and just as deep.

• Know the mature size. Plant based on how big your plants will grow rather than how big they are when you plant them. Large plants should have enough room to mature without interfering with walls, roof overhangs, power lines, walkways or surrounding plants.

• Plant at the same depth. Plants generally like to grow at a certain level in relation to the soil and should be planted at the same level they were at in the pot or container before you transplanted them.

• Identify your plants. Keep track of what's what in your garden by putting a tag next to each plant when you plant it. A gardening journal is a great place to list the plants you have and where you planted them. It is very easy for beginning and seasoned gardeners alike to forget exactly what they planted and where they planted it.

• Water deeply. It's better to water deeply once every week or two, depending on the plant, rather than water a little bit more often. Deep and thorough watering forces roots to grow as they search for water and helps them survive dry spells when water bans may restrict your watering regime. Always check the root zone before you water, as some soils hold more water for longer periods than other soils. More gardeners overwater than underwater. Mulching helps retain moisture and reduces watering needs. Container plantings are the watering exception, as they can quickly dry out and may even need watering every day.

## Choosing Plants

When choosing the plants you want, try to aim for a variety of sizes, shapes, textures, features and bloom times. Features like decorative fruit, variegated or colourful leaves and interesting bark provide interest when plants aren't blooming. This way you will have a garden that captivates your attention all year.

## Annuals

Annuals are planted new each year and are only expected to last for a single growing season. Their flowers and decorative foliage provide bright splashes of colour and can fill in spaces around immature trees, shrubs and perennials.

Annuals are easy to plant and are often sold in small cell-packs of four or six. The roots quickly fill the space in these small

Settle backfilled soil with water.

Water the plant well.

Add a layer of mulch.

Annuals provide colour and flexibility in the garden.

packs, so the small rootball should be broken up before planting. Split the ball in two up the centre or run your thumb up each side to break up the roots.

Many annuals can be grown from seed and are started indoors in March or directly in the garden once the soil begins to warm up.

## Perennials

Perennials come up every year. They usually die back to the ground each fall and send up new shoots in spring, though they can also be evergreen or semi-shrubby. They often have a shorter period of bloom than annuals, but they require less care.

Many perennials benefit from being divided every few years, usually in early spring while plants are still dormant or, in some cases, after flowering. This keeps them growing and blooming

Perennials add colour to beds and borders year after year.

vigorously and, in some cases, controls their spread. Dividing involves digging the plant up, removing dead debris, breaking the plant into several pieces using a sharp knife, spade or saw and replanting some or all of the pieces. Extra pieces can be shared with family, friends and neighbours.

## Trees & Shrubs

Trees and shrubs provide the bones of the garden. They are often the slowest-growing plants but usually live the longest. Characterized by leaf type, they may be deciduous or evergreen, broad-leaved or needled.

Trees should have as little disturbed soil as possible at the bottom of the planting hole. Loose dirt settles over time and sinking even 2.5 cm (1") can

Trees and shrubs are anchors in the landscape.

kill some trees. The prepared area for trees and shrubs needs to be at least two to four times bigger than the root ball.

Staking, sometimes recommended for newly planted trees, is only necessary for trees over 1.5 m (5') tall. Stakes support the rootball until it grows enough to support the tree. Stakes should be short enough to allow the trunk to move with the wind. Rubber inner tubes cut into thin strips make soft and durable ties.

Pruning is more often required for shrubs than for trees. It helps them maintain an attractive shape and can improve blooming. Avoid shearing. Instead, remove the longer branches one by one down to a fork; this is called thinning pruning. The result is a healthy, natural form.

### Roses

Roses are beautiful shrubs with lovely, often fragrant blooms. Traditionally, most roses only bloomed once in the growing season, but new varieties bloom for much longer. Repeat-blooming, or recurrent, roses should be deadheaded to encourage more flower production. One-time bloomers should be left for the colourful hips that develop.

Generally, roses prefer a fertile, well-prepared planting area. A rule of thumb is to prepare an area 60 cm (24") across, front to back and side to side, and 60 cm (24") deep. Add plenty of compost or other fertile organic matter and keep the roses well watered during the growing season. Many roses are quite durable and will adapt to poorer conditions. Grafted roses should be planted with the graft 5 cm (2") below the soil line. When watering, avoid wetting the foliage to reduce the spread of blackspot.

Hybrid roses are challenging to overwinter (though it is possible), but the many hardy shrub roses are as tough as any other shrub.

Roses are lovely on their own or in mixed borders.

Training vines to climb structures adds depth to the garden.

### Vines

Vines or climbing plants are useful for screening and shade, especially in a location too small for a tree. They may be woody or herbaceous and annual or perennial. Vines may physically cling to surfaces, may have wrapping tendrils or stems or may need to be tied in place with string.

Sturdy trellises, arbours, porch railings, fences, walls, poles and trees are all possible vine supports. If a support is needed, ensure it's in place before you plant to avoid disturbing the roots later. Choose a support that is suitable for the vine you are growing. It needs to be sturdy enough to hold the plant up and should match the vine's growing habit—clinging, wrapping or tied.

### Bulbs, Corms & Tubers

These plants have fleshy, underground storage organs that allow them to survive extended periods of dormancy. They are often grown for the bright splashes of colour their flowers provide. They may be spring, summer or fall flowering. Each has an ideal

Crocus in bloom is a harbinger of spring!

depth and time of year at which it should be planted.

Hardy bulbs can be left in the ground and will flower every year. Some popular tender plants are grown from bulbs, corms or tubers and are generally lifted from the garden in late summer or fall as the foliage dies back. These are stored in a cool, frost-free location for winter and then replanted in spring.

## Herbs

Herbs are plants with medicinal, culinary or other economic purposes. A few common culinary herbs are included in this book. Even if you don't cook with them, the often-fragrant foliage adds its aroma to the garden, and the plants can be quite decorative in form, leaf and flower. A conveniently placed container—perhaps near the kitchen door—

Ornamental grasses add colour, variety and texture.

of your favourite herbs will yield plenty of flavour and fragrance all summer.

Many herbs have pollen-producing flowers that attract butterflies, bees, hummingbirds and predatory insects to your garden. Predatory insects feast on problem insects such as aphids, mealy bugs and whiteflies.

## Ferns, Grasses & Groundcovers

Many plants are grown for decorative foliage rather than flowers. Some of these are included in other sections of this book, but we have noted a few with foliage that adds a unique touch to the garden. Ferns, ornamental grasses, groundcovers and other foliage plants bring a variety of colours, textures and forms to the landscape.

Ferns, a common sight in moist and shady gardens, provide a lacy foliage accent and combine well with broad-leaved perennials and shrubs. Some ferns will survive in full sun.

Ornamental grasses and grass-like plants provide interest all year, even in winter when the withered blades are left to stand. Cut them back in early spring and divide them when the clumps begin to die out in the centre.

Groundcovers, although the term can be used to describe any plant, are low-growing plants used to fill in spaces. They suppress weeds, blend plantings together, mask bare ground and provide alternatives to turfgrass where it won't grow or where it's difficult to maintain.

## A Final Comment

The more you discover about the fascinating world of plants, whether from books, talking to other gardeners, appreciating the creative designs of others or experimenting with something new in your own garden, the more rewarding your gardening experience will be. This book is intended as a guide to germinate and grow your passion for plants.

# Ageratum
*Ageratum*

$\mathcal{T}$he fluffy flowers of ageratum, often in shades of blue, add softness and texture to the garden. In the deer zone, this plant can be counted on to be left untouched, like spinach on an eight-year-old's plate!

## Growing
Ageratum prefers **full sun** but tolerates partial shade. The soil should be **fertile, moist** and **well drained**. A moisture-retaining mulch prevents the soil from drying out excessively. Deadhead to prolong blooming and to keep the plants looking tidy.

## Tips
Almost completely covered in flowers when in bloom, the small selections make excellent edging plants for flowerbeds and are attractive when grouped in masses or grown in planters. The tall selections can be included in the centre of a flowerbed and are lovely as cut flowers.

## Recommended
*A. houstonianum* forms a large, leggy mound that can grow up to 75 cm (30") tall. Many cultivars that grow about half as tall, with a low, bushy habit, are available. Flowers are produced in shades of blue, purple, pink or white.

*A. houstonianum* cultivar (above), *A. houstonianum* (below)

*The genus name* Ageratum *is of Greek origin and means "without age," in reference to the long-lasting flowers.*

**Also called:** floss flower **Features:** fuzzy flowers in blue, purple, pink or white; mounded habit **Height:** 15–75 cm (6–30") **Spread:** 15–45 cm (6–18")

# Begonia
*Begonia*

B. *semperflorens* (above), B. x *tuberhybrida* (below)

*Because wax begonias are generally pest free and bloom all summer even without deadheading, they are ideal flowers for the lazy gardener.*

With their beautiful flowers, compact habit and decorative foliage, there is sure to be a begonia to fulfill your shade-gardening needs.

## Growing

**Light shade** or **partial shade** is best, although some wax begonias tolerate sun if the soil is kept moist. The soil should be **neutral to acidic, fertile, rich in organic matter** and **well drained**. Allow the soil to dry out slightly between waterings, particularly for tuberous begonias. Begonias love warm weather, so don't plant them before the soil warms in spring; in cold soil, they may become stunted and fail to thrive.

## Tips

All begonias are useful for shaded garden beds and planters. The trailing, tuberous varieties can be used in hanging baskets and along rock walls, where the flowers can cascade over the edges. Wax begonias have a neat, rounded habit that makes them particularly attractive as edging plants. For a great houseplant over winter, pot either type before the first fall frost.

## Recommended

*B. semperflorens* (wax begonias) have pink, white, red or bicoloured flowers and green, bronze, reddish or white-variegated foliage.

*B. x tuberhybrida* (tuberous begonias) are generally sold as tubers and are popular for their many shades of red, pink, yellow, orange or white flowers.

**Features:** pink, white, red, yellow, orange, bicoloured or picotee flowers; decorative foliage
**Height:** 15–60 cm (6–24")
**Spread:** 15–60 cm (6–24")

# Calendula

## *Calendula*

Bright and charming, calendulas produce attractive, warm-coloured flowers in early summer and again in late summer and fall.

### Growing

Calendula does equally well in **full sun** and **partial shade**. **Well-drained** soil of **average fertility** is preferred. Calendula likes cool weather and can withstand a moderate frost. Sow seed directly in the garden in mid-spring. Deadhead to prolong blooming and to keep the plants looking neat. If the plants get straggly in summer, cut them back to 10–15 cm (4–6") above the ground to promote new growth, or pull them up and seed new ones. Either method provides a good fall display.

### Tips

This informal plant looks attractive in borders and mixed into the vegetable patch. It can also be used in mixed planters.

### Recommended

*C. officinalis* is a vigorous, tough, upright plant that bears daisy-like, single or double flowers in a wide range of yellow and orange shades. Several cultivars are available.

C. officinalis 'Apricot Surprise' (above), C. officinalis (below)

*Calendula is a cold-hardy annual that often continues flowering, even through a layer of snow, until the ground freezes completely.*

**Also called:** pot marigold, English marigold
**Features:** cream, yellow, gold, orange or apricot flowers; long blooming period
**Height:** 25–60 cm (10–24")
**Spread:** 20–50 cm (8–20")

# California Poppy

*Eschscholzia*

*E. californica* (above & below)

A mound of delicate, feathery, blue-green foliage topped with shimmering, satiny flowers in sorbet shades make this annual a repeat favourite.

### Growing

California poppy prefers **full sun**. The soil should be of **poor to average fertility** and **well drained**. Too rich a soil produces lush, green growth but few flowers, if any. This plant tolerates drought once established, but it requires a lot of water for germination and until it begins flowering.

Never start this plant indoors; it dislikes having its roots disturbed. California poppy sprouts quickly when sown directly in the garden in early to mid-spring.

### Tips

California poppy can be included in an annual border or annual planting in a cottage garden. This plant self-seeds wherever it is planted; it is perfect for naturalizing in a meadow garden or rock garden, where it will come back year after year.

### Recommended

*E. californica* forms a mound of delicate, feathery, blue-green foliage. It bears satiny, orange or yellow flowers all summer. Cultivars with semi-double or double flowers and flowers in red, cream, violet or pink are available.

---

**Features:** orange, yellow, red, pink, violet or cream flowers; attractive, feathery foliage
**Height:** 20–45 cm (8–18")
**Spread:** 20–45 cm (8–18")

# China Aster

*Callistephus*

China aster's vividly coloured and densely petalled flowers will steal the spotlight in your garden all summer long, provided you feed and water it adequately.

## Growing

China aster prefers **full sun** but tolerates partial shade. The soil should be **fertile, neutral to alkaline, evenly moist** and **well drained**. If your garden has acidic soil, you may have the best success planting China aster in pots or planters, where the pH is more easily adjusted.

This plant doesn't like to have its roots disturbed, so start the seeds in peat pots or peat pellets. Plant out once the soil has warmed. China aster has shallow roots that can dry out quickly; mulch to conserve moisture.

## Tips

Use small selections as edging plants and tall varieties at the middle and back of the border. Tall selections may require staking or need the support of surrounding plants to prevent them from flopping over. China aster can also be included in mixed containers and planters.

## Recommended

*C. chinensis* is the source of many varieties and cultivars, which come in dwarf, medium and tall height groups.

*C. chinensis* (above & below)

*China aster is a heavy feeder, so you need to fertilize it regularly if you want to enjoy flowers like the ones you see in the gardening catalogues.*

**Features:** purple, blue, pink, red, white, peach or yellow flowers in varied shapes and sizes  **Height:** 30–90 cm (12–36")
**Spread:** 25–45 cm (10–18")

# Cleome

*Cleome*

*C. hassleriana* (above & below)

Create a bold and exotic display in your garden with this lovely and unusual flower. In the deer zone, here's a tall, pink annual they never touch.

## Growing

Cleome prefers **full sun** but tolerates partial shade. It adapts to most soils, although mixing in organic matter to help retain water is a good idea. Cleome tolerates drought but performs best when watered regularly. Pinch out the tip of the centre stem on young plants to encourage branching and more blooms. Deadhead to prolong blooming and to reduce prolific self-seeding.

## Tips

Cleome can be planted in groups at the back of a border or in the centre of an island bed. This striking plant also makes an attractive addition to a large mixed container planting.

## Recommended

*C. hassleriana* is a tall, upright plant with strong, supple, thorny stems. The foliage and flowers of this plant have a strong but not unpleasant scent. Flowers are borne in loose, rounded clusters at the ends of the leafy stems. Many cultivars are available.

**Also called:** spider flower
**Features:** attractive and scented foliage; large, airy, purple, pink or white flowers; thorny stems **Height:** 30 cm–1.5 m (1–5')
**Spread:** 30–60 cm (12–24")

# Coleus

*Solenostemon (Coleus)*

There is a coleus for everyone. From brash yellows, oranges and reds to rosy pinks, deep maroons and almost black selections, the colours, textures and variations are almost limitless.

## Growing

Depending on the cultivar, coleus prefers **light shade** or **partial shade** but tolerates full shade if not too dense and full sun if the plants are watered regularly. The soil should be of **average to rich fertility, humus rich, moist** and **well drained**.

Place the seeds in a refrigerator for one or two days before planting; the low temperatures assist in breaking their dormancy. Press them into the soil surface, but do not cover them because they need light to germinate. Green at first, the seedlings will develop leaf variegation as they mature.

## Tips

The bold, colourful foliage makes coleus a dramatic choice. Group plants together as edging plants or in beds, borders or mixed containers. In a bright room, coleus can also be grown as a houseplant.

When flower buds develop, it is best to pinch them off because the plants tend to stretch out and become less attractive after they flower.

## Recommended

***S. scutellarioides*** (*Coleus blumei* var. *verschaffeltii*) forms a bushy mound of foliage. The leaf edges range from slightly toothed to very ruffled. The

*S. scutellarioides* mixed cultivars (above & below)

leaves are usually multi-coloured, with shades ranging from pale greenish yellow to deep purple-black. Many of the dozens of cultivars available cannot be started from seed.

**Features:** brightly coloured foliage
**Height:** 15–90 cm (6–36") **Spread:** usually equal to height

# Cosmos
*Cosmos*

*E*asy to grow, cosmos are low-cost, low-maintenance, cottage-garden flowers that never fail to delight.

## Growing
Cosmos like **full sun** and **well-drained** soil of **poor to average fertility;** over-watering and overfertilizing can reduce the number of flowers. Plant them out after the last frost. Cut faded blooms to encourage more buds. These plants often self-seed.

## Tips
Cosmos look attractive in a cottage garden, at the back of a border or mass planted in an informal bed. As with many tall annuals, shearing the tops before blooming starts results in bushier, shorter plants that are less likely to topple over.

To stake cosmos plants, push supports, such as twigs, into the ground when the plants are young and allow them to grow up between the branches, hiding their supports. To avoid the need for staking, plant cosmos against a fence or in a sheltered location—or grow short varieties.

## Recommended
*C. bipinnatus* (annual cosmos) is an erect plant with fine, fern-like foliage. It and its many cultivars bear magenta, purple, rose, pink, white or bicoloured flowers, usually with yellow centres.

*C. sulphureus* (yellow cosmos) is a smaller, denser plant than *C. bipinnatus*, and it produces gold, orange, scarlet or yellow flowers. Sow this plant directly in the garden.

*C. bipinnatus* (above & below)

**Features:** magenta, rose, pink, purple, white, yellow, orange, gold, scarlet or bicoloured flowers; fern-like foliage; easy to grow
**Height:** 30 cm–2.1 m (1–7')
**Spread:** 30–45 cm (12–18")

# Dusty Miller
*Senecio*

Dusty miller makes an artful addition to planters, window boxes and mixed borders. Its soft, deeply lobed, silvery grey foliage makes a good backdrop to show off the brightly coloured flowers of other annuals.

## Growing

Dusty miller prefers **full sun** but tolerates light shade. The soil should be of **average fertility** and **well drained**. Like most silver-leafed plants, it is fairly drought resistant.

## Tips

The soft, lacy, silvery leaves of this plant are its main feature. Dusty miller is used primarily as an edging plant, but it is also good in beds, borders and containers.

Pinch off the flowers before they bloom; the flowers aren't showy, and they use energy that would otherwise go to producing more foliage.

Dusty miller holds its own through the early frosts of October and can be used as an important component of attractive fall displays.

## Recommended

**S. cineraria** forms a mound of lobed or finely divided, fuzzy, silvery grey foliage. Many cultivars with impressive foliage colours and shapes have been developed.

*S. cineraria* 'Cirrus' (above), *S. cineraria* (below)

*Mix dusty miller with geraniums, begonias or celosias to complement the vibrant colours of their flowers.*

**Features:** silvery foliage; neat habit
**Height:** 30–60 cm (12–24") **Spread:** equal to height or slightly narrower

# Flowering Cabbage
*Brassica*

B. oleracea cultivar (above & below)

*C*ool nights at the end of summer deepen the colours of this ornamental plant as the days of fall approach.

## Growing

Flowering cabbage prefers **full sun** but tolerates a little bit of shade. The soil should be **fertile, neutral to alkaline, moist** and **well drained**. Plants can be started from seed to flower and develop colourful foliage for the following year or can be purchased in fall to transplant out directly.

Foliage colours develop as the days shorten and intensify once the air temperature falls below 10° C (50° F) or after the first frost.

## Tips

As fall approaches, many gardeners replace faded summer annuals with flowering cabbage. It can be included in beds and borders as well as in mixed containers. Like its vegetable cousins, flowering cabbage attracts cabbage butterfly larvae. Timely application of the biological control BT can prevent serious damage.

## Recommended

*B. oleracea* (Acephala Group) forms loose, upright rosettes of large, often-fringed leaves in shades of purple, red, pink or white.

*Flowering cabbage is a biennial that rarely flowers the first year if grown from seed, which is why, although fully grown, flowering plants are often available in fall.*

**Also called:** ornamental cabbage, flowering kale, ornamental kale **Features:** decorative foliage; cold hardy **Height:** 30–60 cm (12–24") **Spread:** 30–60 cm (12–24")

# Geranium
*Pelargonium*

ough, predictable, sun-loving and drought-resistant, geraniums have earned their place as flowering favourites in the annual garden. If you are looking for something out of the ordinary, seek out the scented geraniums with their fragrant and often decorative foliage.

### Growing
Geraniums prefer **full sun** but tolerate partial shade, although they may not bloom as profusely. The soil should be **fertile** and **well drained**. Deadheading is essential to keep geraniums blooming and looking neat.

### Tips
Very popular, geraniums make useful additions to borders, beds, planters, hanging baskets and window boxes. Treated as annuals, they are actually perennials and can be kept indoors over winter in a bright room. In late winter, take cuttings from these indoor plants to start new plants for the coming season.

### Recommended
*P. peltatum* (ivy-leaved geranium) has thick, waxy leaves and a trailing habit. Many cultivars are available.

*P. zonale* (zonal geranium) is a bushy plant with red, pink, purple, orange or white flowers and, frequently, banded or multi-coloured foliage. Many cultivars are available.

*P. zonale* Fireworks Collection (above), *P. peltatum* (below)

*P.* **species** and **cultivars** (scented geraniums, scented pelargoniums) are grown for their fragrant leaves. The scents are grouped into categories such as rose, mint, citrus, fruit, spice and pungent.

---

**Features:** red, pink, violet, orange, salmon, white, purple or bicoloured flowers; decorative or scented foliage; variable habit
**Height:** 20–60 cm (8–24")
**Spread:** 15 cm–1.2 m (6"–4')

# Heliotrope

*Heliotropium*

*H. arborescens* (above & below)

Heliotrope's big clusters of fragrant flowers on bushy plants have renewed the popularity of this old-fashioned favourite. Pair it with yellow neighbours to create striking contrasts.

## Growing

Heliotrope grows best in **full sun**. The soil should be **fertile, rich in organic matter, moist** and **well drained**. Overwatering can kill heliotrope, but a plant

left to dry to the point of wilting recovers slowly. This cold-sensitive plant should be set outside only after the danger of frost has passed. When early frost is expected in fall, protect heliotrope by covering it or bringing it indoors, where it can be overwintered.

## Tips

Heliotrope is ideal for growing in containers or flowerbeds near windows and patios, where the wonderful fragrance of the flowers can be enjoyed. It can also be grown indoors in a bright, sunny window.

## Recommended

*H. arborescens* is a low, bushy shrub that is usually treated as an annual. It produces large clusters of fragrant flowers in purple, blue or white. Many cultivars are available.

**Also called:** cherry pie plant
**Features:** fragrant flowers in purple, blue or white; attractive foliage **Height:** 45–60 cm (18–24") **Spread:** 30–60 cm (12–24")

# Impatiens
*Impatiens*

mpatiens are the high-wattage dar-lings of the shade garden, delivering masses of flowers in a wide variety of colours. They are perhaps the most reliable of the continually blooming annuals.

## Growing

Impatiens do best in **partial shade** or **light shade** but tolerate full shade or, if kept moist, full sun; New Guinea impatiens are the best adapted to sunny locations. The soil should be **fertile, humus rich, moist** and **well drained**.

## Tips

Impatiens are known and loved for their ability to grow and flower profusely even in shade. Mass plant them in beds under trees, along shady fences or walls or in porch planters. They also look lovely in hanging baskets. New Guinea impatiens are grown as much for their variegated foliage as for their flowers.

## Recommended

*I. hawkeri* (New Guinea hybrids; New Guinea impatiens) flowers in shades of red, orange, pink, purple or white. The foliage is often variegated with a yellow stripe down the centre of each leaf.

*I. walleriana* (impatiens, busy Lizzie) has flowers in shades of purple, red, burgundy, pink, yellow, salmon, orange, apricot, white or bicoloured. Dozens of cultivars are available.

*I. walleriana* (above), *I. hawkeri* (below)

*Impatiens are named for the explosive manner in which the pods split open to expel their seeds, and a number of the common names also refer to this characteristic.*

**Also called:** busy Lizzie, snapweed, touch-me-not **Features:** purple, red, burgundy, pink, yellow, salmon, orange, apricot, white or bicoloured flowers; grows well in shade
**Height:** 15–45 cm (6–18")
**Spread:** 30–60 cm (12–24")

# Lavatera
*Lavatera*

*L. trimestris* 'Silver Cup' (above), *L. trimestris* (below)

$\mathcal{L}$avateras are great plants for tough growing conditions. Many flowers fail in dry, infertile soil, but lavateras just keep blooming, stopping only with the first hard frost of fall.

### Growing
Lavateras prefer **full sun**. The soil should be of **average fertility, light** and **well drained**. These plants like cool, moist weather and shelter from the wind. Sow directly in the garden once the danger of frost has passed. Because lavateras resent having their roots disturbed, use peat pots when starting seeds indoors, then plant out when danger of frost is over.

Stake tall varieties to keep them from flopping over in the rain.

### Tips
These large, shrubby plants work well in beds and borders behind smaller plants for a colourful backdrop—or try planting them as a temporary hedge. The flowers are excellent for cutting and are edible. Although lavateras have no significant insect pests, deer love to nibble the tender flowers.

### Recommended
*L. trimestris* is a bushy plant that bears red, pink, rose, salmon or white, funnel-shaped flowers.

*There are only about 25 species of* Lavatera, *but they comprise a diverse group of annuals, biennials, perennials and shrubs.*

**Also called:** bush mallow, mallow
**Features:** delicate, red, rose, pink, salmon or white flowers; easy to grow; toughness
**Height:** 60 cm–1.2 m (2–4')
**Spread:** 45–60 cm (18–24")

# Licorice Plant
*Helichrysum*

The silvery sheen of licorice plant is caused by a fine, soft pubescence on the leaves. Because silver is the ultimate blending colour, licorice plant is a perfect complement to almost any other plant.

## Growing
Licorice plant prefers **full sun**. The soil should be of **poor to average fertility, neutral to alkaline** and **well drained**. Licorice plant wilts when the soil dries but revives quickly once watered. If it outgrows its space, snip it back with a pair of pruners, shears or even scissors.

## Tips
A perennial grown as an annual, licorice plant is prized for its foliage rather than its flowers. Include it in your hanging baskets, planters and window boxes to provide a soft, silvery backdrop for the colourful flowers of other plants. Licorice plant can also be used as a groundcover in beds, borders and rock gardens or along the tops of retaining walls.

## Recommended
*H. petiolare* is a trailing plant with fuzzy, grey-green leaves. Cultivars are more common than the species and include varieties with lime green, silver or variegated leaves.

H. petiolare 'Silver' (above)
H. petiolare 'Limelight' (below)

*Take cuttings in fall for a supply of new licorice plants the next spring. Once the cuttings have rooted, keep them in a cool, bright location for winter.*

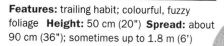

**Features:** trailing habit; colourful, fuzzy foliage **Height:** 50 cm (20") **Spread:** about 90 cm (36"); sometimes up to 1.8 m (6')

# Lobelia

*Lobelia*

Delicate and airy in appearance, lobelia still manages to add a bright splash of colour to the garden.

## Growing

Lobelia grows well in **full sun, partial shade** or **light shade**. The soil should be **fertile, humus rich, moist** and **well drained**. Sun early rather than late in the day is best, and plants in sunny locations need to be kept well watered. Lobelia, which grows best when nights are cool, may fade during hot summer weather.

## Tips

Read the labels carefully when purchasing lobelia plants or seeds—the compact, upright types are useful for edging beds and borders; trailing types hang over the sides of planters, window boxes, mixed containers, hanging baskets and rock walls.

## Recommended

*L. erinus* plants may be rounded and bushy or low and trailing. The flowers are in shades of blue, purple, red, pink or white. The many available cultivars include some recent selections that can better tolerate hot weather.

*L. erinus* 'Sapphire' (above), *L. erinus* cultivars (below)

*Trim back lobelia plants when they begin to fade in summer and keep them well watered. They will revive when the weather cools in late summer and fall.*

**Features:** blue, purple, red, pink or white flowers; airy habit **Height:** 10–25 cm (4–10") **Spread:** 10–25 cm (4–10")

# Marigold
*Tagetes*

From the large, exotic, ruffled flowers of African marigold to the tiny flowers of the low-growing signet marigold, the warm colours and distinctive scent of marigolds add a festive touch to the garden.

## Growing

Marigolds grow best in **full sun**. The soil should be of **average fertility** and **well drained**. These plants tolerate drought and hold up well in windy, rainy weather. Sow seed directly in the garden after the chance of frost has passed. Deadhead to prolong blooming and to keep the plants tidy.

## Tips

Mass planted or mixed with other plants, marigolds make a vibrant addition to beds, borders and container gardens. These plants thrive in the hottest, driest parts of your garden.

## Recommended

Many cultivars are available for all the following species.

*T. erecta* (African marigold, American marigold, Aztec marigold) offers the largest plants with the biggest flowers.

*T. patula* (French marigold) is low growing and has a wide range of flower colours.

*T. tenuifolia* (signet marigold) has become more popular recently because of its feathery foliage and small, dainty flowers.

*T. patula* 'Boy Series' (above), *T. patula* hybrid (below)

*T.* **Triploid Hybrids** (triploid marigold) have been developed by crossing French and African marigolds, which results in plants with large flowers and compact growth.

*Marigolds are often included in vegetable gardens for their reputed insect- and nematode-repelling qualities.*

**Features:** bright yellow, red, orange, brown gold, cream or bicoloured flowers; fragrant foliage **Height:** 15–90 cm (6–36") **Spread:** 30–60 cm (12–24")

# Million Bells
*Calibrachoa*

Million bells are charming and, given the right conditions, bloom continually throughout the growing season.

## Growing
Million bells prefer **full sun**. The soil should be **fertile, moist** and **well drained**. Although they prefer to be watered regularly, million bells are fairly drought resistant once established. They become hardier over summer and, as the weather cools, withstand lower temperatures in fall than they could have in spring.

## Tips
Popular for planters and hanging baskets, million bells are also attractive in beds and borders. They grow all summer and need plenty of room to spread, or they will overtake other flowers. Pinch back to keep the plants compact.

## Recommended
*C.* **hybrids** have a dense, trailing habit. They bear small flowers that look like petunias, and cultivars are available with a wide range of flower colours.

*C.* 'Trailing Blue' (above)
*C.* 'Trailing Pink' and 'Trailing Blue' (below)

Calibrachoa *flowers close at night and on cloudy days.*

---

**Also called:** calibrachoa, trailing petunia
**Features:** pink, purple, yellow, red-orange, white or blue flowers; trailing habit
**Height:** 15–30 cm (6–12") **Spread:** up to 60 cm (24")

# Nasturtium

*Tropaeolum*

*T*hese fast growing, brightly coloured flowers are easy to grow, making them popular with beginners and experienced gardeners alike.

## Growing

Nasturtiums prefer **full sun** but tolerate some shade. The soil should be of **poor to average fertility, light, moist** and **well drained**. Soil that is too rich or has too much nitrogen results in a lot of leaves and very few flowers. Let the soil drain completely between waterings. Sow directly in the garden once the danger of frost has passed.

## Tips

Nasturtiums are used in beds, borders, containers and hanging baskets and on sloped banks. The climbing varieties are grown up trellises or over rock walls or places that need concealing. These plants thrive in poor locations, and they make an interesting addition to plantings on hard-to-mow slopes.

## Recommended

*T. majus* has a trailing habit, but many of the cultivars have bushier, more refined habits. Cultivars offer differing flower colours or variegated foliage.

*T. majus* (above), *T. majus* 'Alaska' (below)

*The leaves and flowers are edible and will add a peppery flavour to salads.*

**Features:** bright red, orange, yellow, burgundy, pink, cream, gold, white or bicoloured flowers; attractive foliage; edible leaves and flowers; varied habits **Height:** 30–45 cm (12–18") for dwarf varieties; up to 3 m (10') for trailing varieties **Spread:** equal to height

# Pansy
*Viola*

*V. x wittrockiana* (above & below)

Colourful and cheerful, pansy flowers are a welcome sight in spring after a long, dreary winter.

## Growing
Pansies prefer **full sun** but tolerate partial shade. The soil should be **fertile, moist** and **well drained**. Pansies do best when the weather is cool, and they may die back a bit over summer. They often rejuvenate in late summer, but it may be easier to pull up faded plants and replace them with new ones in fall. Pansies may very well survive winter and provide you with flowers again the following spring.

## Tips
Pansies can be used in beds and borders, and they are popular for mixing in with spring-flowering bulbs and primroses. They can also be grown in containers.

## Recommended
*V.* **x** *wittrockiana* is a small, bushy plant that bears flowers in a wide range of bright and pastel colours, often with markings near the centres of the petals that give the flowers a face-like appearance.

**Features:** bright or pastel shades of blue, purple, red, orange, yellow, pink or white, often bicoloured or multi-coloured flowers
**Height:** 15–30 cm (6–12")
**Spread:** 15–30 cm (6–12")

# Petunia
*Petunia*

 or speedy growth, prolific blooming and ease of care, petunias are hard to beat. As a bonus, their delicate, sweet perfume permeates the evening air.

## Growing
Petunias prefer **full sun**. The soil should be of **average to rich fertility, light, sandy** and **well drained**. Pinch halfway back in mid-summer to keep the plants bushy and to encourage new growth and flowers.

## Tips
Use petunias in beds, borders, containers and hanging baskets. The best defence against slugs is to encourage plant health with good soil, prompt transplanting and adequate moisture and nutrients.

## Recommended
*P.* x *hybrida* is a large group of popular, sun-loving annuals that fall into three categories. **Grandifloras** have the largest flowers in the widest range of colours, but they can be damaged by rain. **Millifloras** have the smallest flowers in the narrowest range of colours, but this type is the most prolific and least likely to be damaged by heavy rain. **Multifloras** bear intermediate-sized flowers that are only somewhat susceptible to rain damage.

*P. multiflora* type 'Purple Wave' (above)
*P. multiflora* type (below)

*Following the introduction of many new and exciting cultivars, petunias are once again among the most popular and sought-after plants of the annual garden.*

**Features:** pink, purple, red, white, yellow, coral, blue or bicoloured flowers; versatility
**Height:** 15–45 cm (6–18")
**Spread:** 30–60 cm (12–24") or wider

# Poppy
*Papaver*

*P. somniferum* 'Hens and Chickens' (above)
*P. somniferum* 'Peony Flowered' (below)

Poppies look as if they are meant to grow in groups. The many flowers swaying in a breeze, with their often-curving stems, seem to be having lively conversations with one another.

## Growing
Poppies grow best in **full sun**. The soil should be **fertile** and **sandy** with **lots of organic matter** mixed in. **Good drainage** is essential. Direct sow seeds every two weeks in spring. Mix the tiny seeds with fine sand for even sowing. Do not cover—the seeds need light for germination. Deadhead to prolong blooming.

## Tips
Poppies work well in mixed borders where other plants are slow to fill in. After occupying empty spaces early in the season, they die back over summer, leaving room for other plants. Poppies can also be used in rock gardens.

## Recommended
*P. somniferum* (opium poppy) bears often-showy, single or double flowers in red, pink, white or purple. Although, because of its narcotic properties, propagation of the species is restricted in Canada and many other countries, several attractive, permitted cultivars have been developed for ornamental use.

*You may also want to try Oriental poppy (P. orientalis), a lovely perennial with large flowers in shades of red, orange, scarlet, pink or coral.*

**Features:** bright red, pink, white or purple flowers **Height:** 60 cm–1.2 m (2–4') **Spread:** 30 cm (12")

# Snapdragon
## *Antirrhinum*

Snapdragon is among the most appealing of plants. The flower colours are always rich and vibrant, and even the most jaded gardeners are tempted to squeeze open the dragons' mouths.

## Growing
Snapdragon prefers **full sun** but tolerates light shade or partial shade. The soil should be **fertile, rich in organic matter** and **well drained**. This plant prefers a **neutral to alkaline** soil; it does not perform as well in acidic soil. Do not cover the seeds when sowing because they require light for germination.

To encourage bushy growth, pinch the tips of the young plants. As the flower spikes fade, cut them off to promote further blooming and to prevent the plant from dying back before the end of the season.

## Tips
The height of the variety dictates the best place for it in a border—the shortest varieties work well near the front, and the tallest look good in the centre or back. The dwarf and medium-height varieties can also be used in planters. Also available is a trailing variety that makes a lovely addition to hanging baskets, mixed containers and other locations where it has the opportunity to show off its cascading habit.

## Recommended
Many cultivars of **A. *majus*** are available.

**Features:** entertaining flowers in shades of white, cream, yellow, orange, red, maroon, pink or purple; sometimes bicoloured
**Height:** 15 cm–1.2 m (6"–4')
**Spread:** 15–60 cm (6–24")

*A. majus* cultivars (above & below)

They are generally grouped into three size categories: dwarf, medium and giant.

*Snapdragon is a perennial plant that is commonly treated as an annual. Although it won't usually survive winter in our region, it often flowers through much of fall and may self-seed.*

# Sunflower
*Helianthus*

*H. annuus* 'Teddy Bear' (above)
*H. annuus* cultivar (below)

Each of the many sunflower options adds cheerful charm to any garden.

### Growing
Sunflowers grow best in **full sun**. The soil should be of **average fertility, humus rich, moist** and **well drained**. Successive sowings over several weeks in spring prolong the blooming period.

The annual sunflower is an excellent flower for a children's garden. The seeds are big and easy to handle, and they germinate quickly. Until blooming finally occurs, the plants grow continually upward, and their progress can be measured by enthusiastic youngsters.

### Tips
Low-growing varieties can be used in beds, borders and containers. Tall varieties work well at the back of borders and make good screens and temporary hedges. The tallest varieties may need staking.

### Recommended
*H. annuus* has attractive cultivars in a wide range of heights, with single stems or branching habits. The flowers come in a variety of colours, in single to fully double forms.

**Also called:** common sunflower
**Features:** late-summer flowers, most commonly yellow, but also orange, red, brown, cream or bicoloured, typically with brown, purple or rusty red centres; edible seeds **Height:** 40 cm (15") for dwarf varieties; up to 5 m (16') for giant varieties
**Spread:** 30–60 cm (12–24")

# Sweet Alyssum
### *Lobularia*

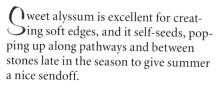

Sweet alyssum is excellent for creating soft edges, and it self-seeds, popping up along pathways and between stones late in the season to give summer a nice sendoff.

## Growing

Sweet alyssum prefers **full sun** but tolerates light shade. **Well-drained** soil of **average fertility** is preferred, but poor soil is tolerated. Sweet alyssum may die back a bit during summer. Trim it back and water it periodically to encourage new growth and more flowers for late summer.

## Tips

Sweet alyssum creeps around rock gardens, over rock walls and along the edges of beds. It is an excellent choice for seeding into cracks and crevices of walkways and between patio stones; once established, it readily reseeds. It is also good for filling in spaces between taller plants in borders and mixed containers.

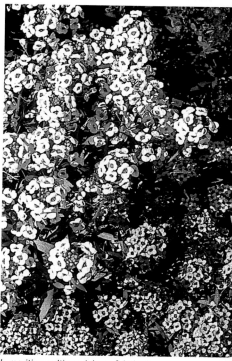

*L. maritima* cultivars (above & below)

## Recommended

**L. maritima** forms a low, spreading mound of foliage. When in full flower, the entire plant appears to be covered in tiny blossoms. Cultivars with flowers in a wide range of colours are available.

*Leave alyssum plants out all winter. In spring, remove the previous year's growth to expose the self-sown seedlings below.*

**Features:** pink, purple, yellow, salmon or white, fragrant flowers  **Height:** 5–30 cm (2–12")
**Spread:** 15–60 cm (6–24")

# Sweet Potato Vine

*Ipomoea*

This vigorous, rambling plant with leaves of lime green, bruised purple or a variegated green, pink and cream can make any gardener look like a genius.

### Growing
Grow sweet potato vine in **full sun**. A **light, well-drained** soil of **poor fertility** is preferred, but any type of soil will do.

### Tips
Sweet potato vine is a great addition to mixed planters, window boxes and hanging baskets. In a rock garden, it scrambles about, and it happily cascades over the edge when planted atop a retaining wall. Although this plant is a vine, its bushy habit and colourful leaves make it a useful foliage plant. Pairing the chartreuse and purple varieties in one container provides a striking contrast.

### Recommended
*I. batatas* (sweet potato vine) is a twining climber that is grown for its attractive foliage rather than its flowers. Several cultivars are available.

*I. batatas* 'Blackie' (above)
*I. batatas* 'Margarita' (below)

*As a bonus when you pull up your plant at the end of summer, you can eat any tubers (sweet potatoes) that have formed.*

**Features:** decorative foliage  **Height:** about 30 cm (12")  **Spread:** up to 3 m (10')

# Treasure Flower

*Gazania*

*G. rigens* cultivars (above), *G. rigens* (below)

Few other flowers can rival treasure flower for adding vivid oranges, reds and yellows to the garden.

## Growing

Treasure flower grows best in **full sun** but tolerates some shade. The soil should be of **poor to average fertility, sandy** and **well drained**. Treasure flower tolerates drought and grows best when temperatures climb over 25° C (75° F). The flowers may stay open only on sunny days.

## Tips

Low-growing treasure flower makes an excellent groundcover and is also useful on exposed slopes, in mixed containers and as an edging plant in flowerbeds. It is a wonderful addition to a xeriscape or dry garden design.

## Recommended

*G. rigens* forms a low basal rosette of lobed foliage. Large, daisy-like flowers with pointed petals are borne on strong stems above the foliage. Many cultivars are available.

*This native of southern Africa has very few pests or problems and transplants easily, even when blooming.*

**Also called:** gazania  **Features:** red, orange, yellow, pink or cream flowers  **Height:** usually 15–20 cm (6–8"); may reach 30–45 cm (12–18")  **Spread:** 20–30 cm (8–12")

# Verbena
*Verbena*

*V. bonariensis* (above), *V. x hybrida* (below)

Verbenas offer butterflies a banquet. Butterfly visitors include tiger swallowtails, silver-spotted skippers, great spangled fritillaries and painted ladies.

## Growing

Verbenas grow best in **full sun**. The soil should be **fertile** and **very well drained**. Pinch back young plants for bushy growth.

*If your verbenas become leggy or overgrown, cut them back by one-half to tidy them up and to promote the production of prolific fall blooms.*

## Tips

Use verbenas on rock walls and in beds, borders, rock gardens, containers, hanging baskets and window boxes. They make good substitutes for ivy-leaved geraniums where the sun is hot and where a roof overhang keeps the mildew-prone verbenas dry.

## Recommended

*V. bonariensis* forms a low clump of foliage from which tall, stiff stems bear clusters of small, purple flowers.

*V. x hybrida* is a bushy plant that may be upright or spreading. It bears clusters of small flowers in a wide range of colours. Cultivars are available.

---

**Also called:** garden verbena **Features:** red, pink, purple, blue, yellow, scarlet, silver, peach or white flowers, sometimes with white centres **Height:** 20 cm–1.5 m (8"–5') **Spread:** 30–90 cm (12–36")

# Ajuga
*Ajuga*

Often labeled as rampant runners, ajugas grow best where they can roam freely. Although some species and cultivars are considered invasive, there are well-behaved cultivars available.

## Growing
Ajugas develop the best leaf colour in **partial shade** or **light shade** but tolerate full shade. The leaves may become scorched when exposed to too much sun. Any **well-drained** soil is suitable. Divide these vigorous plants any time during the growing season.

Remove any new growth or seedlings that don't show the hybrid leaf colouring.

## Tips
Ajugas make excellent groundcovers for difficult sites, such as exposed slopes and dense shade. They are also attractive in shrub borders, where their dense growth will prevent the spread of all but the most tenacious weeds.

## Recommended
*A. pyramidalis* 'Metallica Crispa' (upright bugleweed) is a very slow-growing plant with bronzy, crinkly foliage and violet-blue flowers.

*A. reptans* is a low, quick-spreading groundcover. The many cultivars are grown for their colourful, often variegated foliage. One of the most popular cultivars is **'Burgundy Glow,'** with a dense and compact habit and foliage variegated in shades of bronze, green, white and pink.

**Also called:** bugleweed **Features:** late-spring to early-summer, purple, blue, pink or white flowers; colourful foliage **Height:** 5–30 cm (2–12") **Spread:** 15–90 cm (6–36") **Hardiness:** zones 3–8

*A. reptans* (above), *A. reptans* cultivar (below)

*The colourful foliage creates a striking contrast when combined with white- or yellow-flowered plants.*

# Artemisia

*Artemisia*

A. *schmidtiana* 'Nana' (above)
A. *ludoviciana* 'Valerie Finnis' (below)

M ost artemisias are valued for their silvery foliage, not their flowers. Silver is the ultimate blending colour in the garden because it enhances every other hue combined with it.

## Growing

Artemisias grow best in **full sun**. The soil should be of **low to average fertility** and **well drained**. Adapted to arid regions, these plants dislike wet, humid conditions.

When artemisias begin to look straggly, cut them back hard to encourage new growth and to maintain a neater form. Divide them every year or two when plant clumps appear to be thinning in the centres.

## Tips

Use artemisias in rock gardens and borders. Their silvery grey foliage makes them good backdrop plants to use behind brightly coloured flowers. They are also useful for filling in spaces between other plants. Smaller forms may be used to create knot gardens. Some varieties can spread and become invasive in the garden.

## Recommended

A. *ludoviciana* (white sage, silver sage) is an upright, clump-forming plant with silvery white foliage. The species is rarely grown in favour of its many cultivars including **'Silver King'** and **'Silver Queen.'** (Zones 4–8)

A. x **'Powis Castle'** is a compact, mounding, shrubby plant with feathery, silvery grey foliage. This hybrid is reliably hardy to zone 6, but it can also grow in colder regions if provided with winter protection and a sheltered location.

A. *schmidtiana* (silvermound artemisia) is a low, dense, mound-forming, non-invasive perennial with feathery, hairy, silvery grey foliage. **'Nana'** (dwarf silvermound) is very compact and grows only half the size of the species. (Zones 4–8)

**Also called:** wormwood, sage **Features:** silvery grey, feathery or deeply lobed foliage **Height:** 15 cm–1.8 m (6"–6') **Spread:** 30–90 cm (12–36") **Hardiness:** zones 3–8

# Astilbe

*Astilbe*

*A.* x *arendsii* cultivars (above), *A.* x *arendsii* 'Bressingham Beauty' (below)

A stilbes are beacons in the shade. Their high-impact flowers will brighten any gloomy section of your garden.

## Growing

Astilbes grow best in **light shade** or **partial shade**. They tolerate full shade, though with fewer flowers, and full sun, if you build deep, humus-rich soil that holds plenty of moisture. The soil should be **fertile, humus rich, acidic, moist** and **well drained**. Although astilbes appreciate moist soil, they don't like standing water.

Astilbes should be divided every three years or so to maintain plant vigour. Root masses may lift out of the soil as they mature. Add a layer of topsoil and mulch if this occurs.

## Tips

Astilbes can be grown near the edges of bog gardens and ponds and in woodland gardens and shaded borders.

## Recommended

*A.* **x** *arendsii* (astilbe, false spirea, Arend's astilbe) is a group of hybrids with many available cultivars.

*A. chinensis* (Chinese astilbe) is a dense, vigorous perennial that tolerates dry soil better than other astilbe species. Many cultivars are available.

*A. japonica* (Japanese astilbe) is a compact, clump-forming perennial. The species is rarely grown in favour of the many cultivars.

**Features:** attractive foliage; white, pink, purple, peach or red, summer flowers
**Height:** 25 cm–1.2 m (10"–4') **Spread:** 20–90 cm (8–36") **Hardiness:** zones 3–8

# Basket-of-Gold
*Aurinia*

*A. saxatilis* (above & below)

This bright yellow harbinger of spring is another on the long list of plants that are a welcome sight after a long, cold winter.

### Growing
Basket-of-gold grows best in **full sun**. The soil should be of **poor to average fertility, sandy** and **well drained**. Plants are drought tolerant and may rot in wet soil and become floppy in too fertile soil. Plants resent having their roots disturbed and should not be moved or divided.

Shear basket-of-gold back lightly after flowering to keep plants compact and to perhaps encourage a few more flowers. Its single, semi-woody main stem makes traditional division impossible. Plants may self seed and new plants can be propagated from stem cuttings of new growth.

### Tips
Basket-of-gold is useful in borders and rock gardens, along retaining wall tops and as a groundcover in difficult or little-used areas. Avoid planting it near slow-growing companions, as basket-of-gold can quickly overwhelm them.

### Recommended
*A. saxatilis* is a vigorous, mound-forming perennial with bright yellow flowers. There are several cultivars available, offering features such as compact growth, apricot-coloured flowers or variegated foliage.

**Features:** spring flowers in shades of yellow or apricot; low-growing, spreading habit **Height:** 15–30 cm (6–12") **Spread:** 20–45 cm (8–18") **Hardiness:** zones 3–7

# Beebalm

*Monarda*

Beebalm will bring visitors of many descriptions to your garden. Butterflies, bees, hummingbirds, moths, colourful flies and others will come for the nectar of this vigorous summer bloomer.

## Growing

Beebalm grows well in **full sun, partial shade** and **light shade**. The soil should be of **average fertility, humus rich, moist** and **well drained**. Dry conditions and poor air circulation encourage mildew and leaf loss. Keep plants well watered. Divide in spring as new growth emerges, when clumps appear to be thinning in the middle.

If you've found mildew to be a problem in the past, try thinning the stems out by a quarter or a third in spring or early summer.

## Tips

Beebalm makes a lovely addition to a garden next to a pond or stream or in a sunny or lightly shaded, well-watered border. As these plants attract bees, butterflies and hummingbirds, you should avoid using pesticides or other chemicals that could harm or kill these creatures.

## Recommended

*M. didyma* is a bushy, mounding plant with red, pink or purple flowers. Cultivars like **'Gardenview Scarlet,'** with red flowers, and **'Marshall's Delight,'** with pink flowers, are desirable because they are resistant to powdery mildew.

M. didyma 'Marshall's Delight' (above)
M. didyma (below)

**Also called:** bergamot, Oswego tea
**Features:** red, pink or purple, mid-summer flowers; fragrant foliage; bushy habit
**Height:** 60 cm–1.2 m (2–4')
**Spread:** 30–60 cm (12–24")
**Hardiness:** zones 3–8

# Bellflower
*Campanula*

C. carpatica (above), C. carpatica 'White Clips' (below)

Thanks to their wide range of heights and habits, it is possible to put bell-flowers almost anywhere in the garden.

*Divide bellflowers every few years, in early spring or late summer, to keep plants vigorous and to prevent them from becoming invasive.*

## Growing

Bellflowers grow well in **full sun, partial shade** or **light shade**. The soil should be of **average to high fertility** and **well drained**. These plants appreciate a mulch to keep their roots cool and moist in summer and protected from fluctuating temperatures in winter. Deadhead to prolong blooming.

## Tips

Plant upright and mounding bellflowers in borders and cottage gardens. Use low, spreading and trailing bellflowers in rock gardens and on rock walls. You can also edge beds with the low-growing varieties.

## Recommended

*C.* x **'Birch Hybrid'** is a low-growing and spreading plant. It bears light blue to mauve flowers in summer.

*C. carpatica* (Carpathian bellflower, Carpathian harebell) is a spreading, mounding perennial that bears blue, white or purple flowers in summer. Several cultivars are available.

*C. glomerata* (clustered bellflower) forms a clump of upright stems and bears clusters of purple, blue or white flowers throughout most of summer.

*C. persicifolia* (peachleaf bellflower) is an upright perennial that bears white, blue or purple flowers from early to mid-summer. **'Alba'** is a white-flowered cultivar.

**Also called:** campanula **Features:** blue, white, purple or pink, spring, summer or fall flowers; varied growing habits
**Height:** 10 cm–1.8 m (4"–6')
**Spread:** 30–90 cm (12–36")
**Hardiness:** zones 3–7

# Blazing Star

*Liatris*

Blazing star is an outstanding cut flower with fuzzy, spiked blossoms above grass-like foliage. It is also an excellent plant for attracting butterflies to the garden.

## Growing

Blazing star prefers **full sun**. The soil should be of **average fertility, sandy** and **humus rich**. Water well during the growing season, but don't allow the plants to stand in water during cool weather. Mulching during summer will reduce moisture loss.

Remove spikes as they fade to prolong the blooming period and to keep plants looking tidy. Divide in fall every three or four years when the clump begins to look crowded.

## Tips

Use this plant in borders and meadow plantings. Plant in a location that has good drainage to avoid root rot during winter. Blazing star grows well in planters.

## Recommended

**L. spicata** is a clump-forming, erect plant with pinkish purple or white flowers. Several cultivars are available.

*The spikes of blazing star make long-lasting cut flowers.*

*L. spicata* 'Kobold' (above), *L. spicata* (below)

**Also called:** liatris, spike gayfeather, gayfeather  **Features:** purple or white, summer flowers; grass-like foliage  **Height:** 45–90 cm (18–36")  **Spread:** 45–60 cm (18–24")  **Hardiness:** zones 3–8

# Bleeding Heart

*Dicentra*

*D. formosa* (above), *D. spectabilis* (below)

Every garden should have a spot for bleeding hearts. Tucked away in a shady spot, these lovely plants appear in spring and fill the garden with fresh promise.

*All bleeding hearts contain toxic alkaloids, and some people develop allergic skin reactions from contact with these plants.*

## Growing

Bleeding hearts prefer **light shade** but tolerate partial shade or full shade. The soil should be **humus rich, moist** and **well drained**. Very dry summer conditions cause the plants to die back, though they will revive in fall or the following spring. Bleeding hearts should be kept moist while blooming in order to prolong the flowering period. Regular watering will keep the flowers coming until mid-summer.

## Tips

Bleeding hearts can be naturalized in a woodland garden or grown in a border or rock garden. They make excellent early-season specimen plants and do well near ponds or streams. Trim back common bleeding heart during and after bloom to control its sprawling form and to encourage compact growth.

## Recommended

*D. eximia* (fringed bleeding heart) forms a loose, mounded clump of lacy, fern-like foliage and bears pink or white flowers in spring and sporadically over summer.

*D. formosa* (western bleeding heart) is a low-growing, wide-spreading plant with pink flowers that fade to white as they mature. The most drought tolerant of the bleeding hearts, it is the most likely to continue flowering all summer.

*D. spectabilis* (common bleeding heart, Japanese bleeding heart) forms a large, elegant mound that bears flowers with white inner petals and pink outer petals. Several cultivars are available.

**Features:** pink, white, red or purple, spring and summer flowers; attractive foliage **Height:** 30 cm–1.2 m (1–4') **Spread:** 30–90 cm (12–36") **Hardiness:** zones 3–8

# Bugbane
## *Actaea (Cimicifuga)*

Bugbanes put on impressive displays. These tall plants bear fragrant flowers above decorative foliage.

## Growing

Bugbanes grow best in **partial shade** or **light shade**. The soil should be **fertile, humus rich** and **moist**. The plants may require support from a peony hoop. They spread by rhizomes; small pieces of root can be carefully unearthed and replanted in spring if more plants are desired.

## Tips

Bugbanes make attractive additions to an open woodland garden, shaded border or pondside planting. They don't compete well with tree roots or other plants that have vigorous roots. Bugbanes are worth growing close to the house because the late-season flowers are wonderfully fragrant.

## Recommended

*A. racemosa* (black snakeroot) is a clump-forming perennial with long-stemmed spikes of fragrant, creamy white flowers. **'Atropurpurea'** has purple foliage and creates a striking focal point in the garden.

A. racemosa (above & below)

*A. racemosa is also known as black cohosh, and the rhizomes are used in herbal medicine.*

---

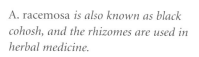

**Also called:** snakeroot **Features:** fragrant, white, cream or pink, late-summer and fall flowers; some with bronze or purple foliage **Height:** 90 cm–2.7 m (3–9') **Spread:** 60 cm (24") **Hardiness:** zones 3–8

# Columbine

*Aquilegia*

A. *canadensis* (above)
A. x *hybrida* 'McKana Giants' (below)

Delicate and beautiful columbines add a touch of simple elegance to any garden. Blooming from spring through mid-summer, these long-lasting flowers herald the passage of cool spring weather and the arrival of warm summer weather.

## Growing

Columbines grow well in **light shade** or **partial shade**. They prefer soil that is **fertile, moist** and **well drained** but adapt to most soil conditions. Division is not required but can be done to propagate desirable plants. The divided plants may take a while to recover because columbines dislike having their roots disturbed.

## Tips

Use columbines in rock gardens, formal or casual borders and naturalized or woodland gardens. This is a short-lived perennial, so plan to add new ones as old plants disappear.

## Recommended

*A. canadensis* (wild columbine, Canada columbine) is a native plant that is common in woodlands and fields. It bears yellow flowers with red spurs.

*A. x hybrida* (*A.* x *cultorum*; hybrid columbine) forms mounds of delicate foliage and has exceptional flowers. Many hybrids have been developed with showy flowers in a wide range of colours.

*A. vulgaris* (European columbine, common columbine) has been used to develop many hybrids and cultivars with flowers in a variety of colours.

*Columbines self-seed but are not invasive. Each year a few new seedlings may turn up near the parent plant and can be transplanted.*

**Features:** red, yellow, pink, purple, blue or white, spring and summer flowers; colour of spurs often differs from that of petals; attractive foliage **Height:** 45–90 cm (18–36") **Spread:** 30–60 cm (12–24") **Hardiness:** zones 3–8

# Coreopsis

*Coreopsis*

*C. verticillata* 'Moonbeam' (above), *C. verticillata* (below)

These plants produce flowers all summer and are easy to grow; they make a fabulous addition to every garden.

## Growing

Coreopsis grows best in **full sun**. The soil should be of **average fertility, sandy, light** and **well drained**. Plants can develop crown rot in moist, cool locations with heavy soil. Too fertile a soil will encourage floppy growth. Deadhead to keep plants blooming.

## Tips

Coreopsis plants are versatile, useful in formal and informal borders and in meadow plantings and cottage gardens. They look best when planted in groups.

## Recommended

*C. verticillata* (thread-leaf coreopsis) is a mound-forming plant with attractive, finely divided foliage and bright yellow flowers. It grows 60–80 cm (24–32") tall and spreads 45 cm (18"). One of the best known cultivars is **'Moonbeam,'** which forms a mound of delicate, lacy foliage, bears creamy yellow flowers and was Perennial Plant of the Year in 1992.

*Mass plant coreopsis to fill in a dry, exposed bank where nothing else will grow, and enjoy the bright sunny flowers all summer long.*

**Also called:** tickseed **Features:** yellow, summer flowers; attractive foliage **Height:** 60–80 cm (24–32") **Spread:** 30–60 cm (12–24") **Hardiness:** zones 3–8

# Daylily
## *Hemerocallis*

He daylily's adaptability and durability, combined with its variety in colour, blooming period, size and texture, explain this perennial's popularity.

### Growing

Daylilies grow in any light from **full sun to full shade**. The deeper the shade, the fewer flowers will be produced. The soil should be **fertile, moist** and **well drained**, but these plants adapt to most conditions and are hard to kill once established. Divide every two to three years to keep the plants vigorous and to propagate them. They can, however, be left indefinitely without dividing.

### Tips

Plant daylilies alone, or group them in borders, on banks and in ditches to control erosion. They can be naturalized in woodland or meadow gardens. Small varieties are nice in planters.

### Recommended

Daylilies come in an almost infinite number of forms, sizes and flower colours in a range of species, cultivars and hybrids. See your local garden centre or daylily grower to find out what's available. Ask for field-grown daylilies, as they adapt quickly.

*H. 'Dewey Roquemore' (above), H. 'Bonanza' (below)*

*Deadhead to prolong the blooming period. Be careful when deadheading purple-flowered daylilies because the sap can stain fingers and clothes.*

**Features:** spring and summer flowers in every colour except blue and pure white; grass-like foliage **Height:** 30 cm–1.2 m (1–4') **Spread:** 30 cm–1.2 m (1–4') **Hardiness:** zones 2–8

# Dead Nettle

*Lamium*

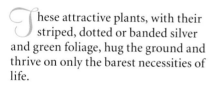

These attractive plants, with their striped, dotted or banded silver and green foliage, hug the ground and thrive on only the barest necessities of life.

## Growing

Dead nettles prefer **partial to light shade**. They tolerate full sun but may become leggy. The soil should be of **average fertility, humus rich, moist** and **well drained**. The more fertile the soil, the more vigorously the plants will grow. These plants are drought tolerant when grown in the shade but can develop bare patches if the soil is allowed to dry out for extended periods. Divide and replant them in fall if the bare spots become unsightly.

Dead nettles remain more compact if sheared back after flowering. If they remain green over winter, shear them back in early spring.

## Tips

These plants make useful groundcovers for woodland or shade gardens. Dead nettles also work well under shrubs in a border, where they will keep weeds down. These plants can spread and become invasive in the garden.

## Recommended

*L. galeobdolon* (*Lamiastrum galeobdolon*; yellow archangel) can be quite invasive, though the cultivars are less so. The flowers are yellow and bloom from spring to early summer.

*L. maculatum* 'Lime Light' (above)
*L. maculatum* 'Beacon Silver' (below)

*L. maculatum* (spotted dead nettle, lamium) is the most commonly grown dead nettle. This low-growing, spreading species has green leaves with white or silvery markings and bears white, pink or mauve flowers. Many cultivars are available.

**Features:** spring or summer flowers in white, pink, yellow or mauve; decorative, often variegated foliage **Height:** 10–60 cm (4–24") **Spread:** indefinite **Hardiness:** zones 3–8

# Drumstick Primrose

*Primula*

*P. denticulata* (above & below)

Planted among dwarf daffodils and lungworts, primroses add to the tapestry of woodland flowers in springtime.

## Growing

Grow drumstick primrose in **light shade** or **partial shade**. The soil should be **moderately fertile, humus rich, neutral** to acidic, moist and **well drained**. Divide after flowering or in early fall when clumps become overgrown.

## Tips

Drumstick primrose makes a lovely addition to lightly shaded borders or even sunny borders if it is grown beneath shrubby or taller companions. It can also be included in woodland gardens, where it looks good in small groups or mass-planted.

## Recommended

*P. denticulata* forms a rosette of spoon-shaped leaves that are powdery white on the undersides. The early- to late-spring flowers are borne in dense, ball-like clusters atop thick stems.

**Also called:** Himalayan primrose
**Features:** purple, white, pink or red, yellow-centred, spring flowers **Height:** 30–45 cm (12–18") **Spread:** 25–30 cm (10–12")
**Hardiness:** zones 2–8

# False Indigo
*Baptisia*

Spikes of bright blue flowers in early summer and attractive, green foliage make this plant a worthy addition, even if it does take up a sizeable amount of garden real estate.

## Growing

False indigo prefers **full sun** but tolerates partial shade. Too much shade causes lank growth that flops over easily. The soil should be of **poor to average fertility, sandy** and **well drained**. False indigo shouldn't be divided and resents transplanting, as it doesn't like having its roots disturbed.

## Tips

False indigo can be used in an informal border or cottage garden. It is an attractive addition for a naturalized planting, on a slope or in any sunny, well-drained spot in the garden.

## Recommended

***B. australis*** is an upright or somewhat spreading, clump-forming plant that bears spikes of purple-blue flowers in early summer.

*B. australis* 'Purple Smoke' (above), *B. australis* (below)

*If you've had difficulties growing lupine, try the far less demanding false indigo instead.*

**Features:** purple-blue, late-spring or early-summer flowers; attractive habit and foliage **Height:** 90 cm–1.5 m (3–5') **Spread:** 60 cm–1.2 m (2–4') **Hardiness:** zones 3–8

# Foamflower

*Tiarella*

*T. cordifolia* (above & below)

Foamflowers, with attractive leaves and delicate, starry, white flowers, form handsome groundcovers in shaded areas.

## Growing

Foamflowers prefer **partial shade, light shade** or **full shade** without afternoon sun. The soil should be **humus rich, moist** and **slightly acidic**. These plants adapt to most soils. Divide in spring. Deadhead to encourage reblooming. If the foliage fades or develops rust in summer, cut it partway to the ground and new growth will emerge.

## Tips

Foamflowers are excellent groundcovers for shaded and woodland gardens. They can be included in shaded borders and left to naturalize in wild gardens.

## Recommended

There are many hybrid foamflowers available, many with very decorative, variegated foliage.

*T. cordifolia* is a low-growing, spreading plant that bears spikes of foamy-looking, white flowers. Cultivars are available.

*T. wherryii* (Wherry's foamflower) forms a slow-growing clump of heart-shaped, lobed, purple-tinged, light green foliage. Star-shaped, pink-tinged or white flowers are produced on spikes in spring and early summer.

**Features:** white or pink, spring and sometimes early-summer flowers; decorative foliage **Height:** 10–30 cm (4–12") **Spread:** 20–60 cm (8–24") **Hardiness:** zones 3–8

# Foxglove
## *Digitalis*

oxglove self-seeds happily and often pops up in new combinations with other plants. Its tubular flowers with spotted landing pads are perfectly adapted to pollination by bumblebees.

## Growing

Foxglove grows well in **partial shade** or **light shade** in **moist, fertile, humus-rich** soil. It adapts to most soils that are neither too wet nor too dry. Plants in windy locations may need staking.

If you allow a few flower spikes to produce seeds, foxglove will self-seed and continue to inhabit your garden. Extra seedlings can be thinned out or transplanted to a new location—perhaps a friend's garden.

## Tips

Foxglove is a biennial grown as a short-lived perennial. Sow seed directly, plant cell packs in fall or purchase larger plants in spring that will bloom that summer. Foxglove makes an excellent vertical accent along the middle to back of a border and is an interesting addition to woodland gardens with filtered light.

*D. purpurea* (above & below)

## Recommended

**D. purpurea** forms a basal rosette of foliage from which tall, flowering spikes in a wide range of colours emerge. The flowers often have contrasting freckles and spots on the inside. **Excelsior Hybrids** bear dense spikes of flowers. **Foxy Hybrids** are considered dwarf by foxglove standards.

*All parts of this plant are poisonous; wear gloves when handling it and wash your hands thoroughly afterward.*

**Features:** attractive pink, purple, yellow, maroon, red or white, spring to early-summer flowers; attractive growth habit **Height:** 60 cm–1.5 m (2–5') **Spread:** 30–60 cm (12–24") **Hardiness:** zones 3–8

# Globe Thistle

*Echinops*

Globe thistle makes a striking choice for gardeners who need a large, low-maintenance specimen to fill an unused corner.

## Growing

Globe thistle prefers **full sun** but tolerates partial shade. The soil should be of **poor to average fertility** and **well drained**. Divide in spring when the clump appears dense and overgrown. Wear gloves and long sleeves to protect yourself from the prickles when dividing. Deadhead to keep plants tidy and to reduce self-seeding.

## Tips

Globe thistle is a striking plant for the back or centre of a border and for neglected areas of the garden that are often missed when watering.

## Recommended

*E. ritro* forms a compact clump of spiny foliage with perfectly globular 5 cm (2") steely blue flowers on 90 cm–1.5 m (3–5') stalks.

*E. ritro* (above & below)

*If you cut your plant back after the first flush of blooms wanes, you may find your globe thistle beginning to bloom again in late summer.*

**Also called:** small globe thistle
**Features:** purple or blue, summer flowers; spiny foliage; clump-forming habit
**Height:** 60 cm–1.5 m (2–5') **Spread:** 60 cm (24") **Hardiness:** zones 3–8

# Goat's Beard

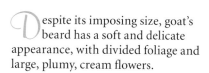

*Aruncus*

Despite its imposing size, goat's beard has a soft and delicate appearance, with divided foliage and large, plumy, cream flowers.

## Growing

These plants prefer **partial to full shade**. If planted in deep shade, they bear fewer blooms. They will tolerate full sun as long as the soil is kept evenly moist and they are protected from the afternoon sun. The soil should be **fertile, moist** and **humus rich**.

## Tips

These plants look very natural growing near the sunny entrance or edge of a woodland garden, in a native plant garden or in a large island planting. They may also be used in a border or alongside a stream or pond.

## Recommended

*A. aethusifolius* (dwarf Korean goat's beard) forms a low-growing, compact mound and bears branched spikes of loosely held, cream flowers.

*A. dioicus* (giant goat's beard, common goat's beard) forms a large, bushy, shrub-like perennial with large plumes of creamy white flowers. There are several cultivars.

*A. dioicus* (above & below)

*Male and female flowers are produced on separate plants. In general, male flowers are full and fuzzy while female flowers are more pendulous, but it can be difficult to tell the two apart.*

**Features:** cream or white, early- to mid-summer blooms; shrub-like habit; attractive foliage and seedheads **Height:** 15 cm–1.8 m (6"–6') **Spread:** 60 cm–1.8 m (2–6') **Hardiness:** zones 3–7

# Hardy Geranium

*Geranium*

G. sanguineum var. striatum (above)
G. sanguineum (below)

There is a type of geranium that suits every garden, thanks to the beauty and diversity of this hardy plant.

## Growing

Hardy geraniums grow well in **full sun, partial shade** and **light shade**. These plants dislike hot weather and prefer soil of **average fertility** and **good drainage**. *G. renardii* prefers a poor, well-drained soil. Divide in spring.

## Tips

These long-flowering plants are great in a border; they fill in the spaces between shrubs and other larger plants and keep the weeds down. They can be included in rock gardens and woodland gardens or mass planted as groundcovers.

## Recommended

**G. 'Brookside'** is a clump-forming, drought-tolerant geranium with finely cut leaves and deep blue to violet-blue flowers.

**G. cinereum** 'Ballerina' forms a basal rosette of silvery green foliage. It produces small clusters of pink flowers with dark purple veins.

**G. macrorrhizum** (bigroot geranium, scented cranesbill) forms a spreading mound of fragrant foliage and bears flowers in various shades of pink. Cultivars are available.

**G. sanguineum** (bloodred cranesbill, bloody cranesbill) forms a dense, mounding clump and bears bright magenta flowers. Many cultivars are available.

*If the foliage looks tatty in late summer, prune it back to rejuvenate it.*

**Also called:** cranesbill geranium **Features:** white, red, pink, purple or blue, summer flowers; attractive, sometimes fragrant foliage **Height:** 10–90 cm (4–36") **Spread:** 60–90 cm (24–36") **Hardiness:** zones 3–8

# Heuchera

*Heuchera*

From soft yellow-greens and oranges to midnight purples and silvery, dappled maroons, heucheras offer a great variety of foliage options for a perennial garden with partial shade.

## Growing

Heucheras grow best in **light shade** or **partial shade** and tolerate full sun, though some foliage colours may bleach out. Plants grow leggy in full shade. The soil should be of **average to rich fertility, humus rich, neutral to alkaline, moist** and **well drained**. Good air circulation is essential. Deadhead to prolong blooming. Every three or four years, heucheras should be dug up and the oldest, woodiest roots and stems removed. Plants may be divided at this time, if desired, then replanted with the crown at or just above soil level.

## Tips

Grown for their foliage more than their flowers, heucheras are useful individually or in groups as edging plants, in woodland gardens or as groundcovers in low-traffic areas. Combine different foliage types for an interesting display.

## Recommended

There are dozens of beautiful cultivars available with almost limitless variations of foliage markings and colours. See your local garden centre or mail-order catalogue to see what is available.

*H. x brizoides* 'Firefly' (above), *H. sanguineum* (below)

*Heucheras have a strange habit of pushing themselves up out of the soil because of their shallow root systems. Mulch in fall if the plants begin heaving from the ground.*

**Also called:** coralbells, alumroot **Features:** very decorative foliage; red, pink, white, yellow or purple, spring or summer flowers **Height:** 30–60 cm (12–24") **Spread:** 15–45 cm (6–18") **Hardiness:** zones 3–8

# Hosta

*Hosta*

*H.* 'Francee' (above)

reeders are always looking for new variations in hosta foliage. Swirls, stripes, puckers and ribs enhance the leaves' various sizes, shapes and colours.

## Growing

Hostas prefer **light shade** or **partial shade** but will grow in full shade. Morning sun is preferable to afternoon sun in partial shade situations. The soil should ideally be **fertile, moist** and **well drained**, but most soils are tolerated. Hostas are fairly drought tolerant, especially if given a mulch to help retain moisture.

Division is not required but can be done every few years in spring or summer to propagate new plants.

## Tips

Hostas make wonderful woodland plants and look very attractive when combined with ferns and other fine-textured plants. Hostas are also good plants for a mixed border, particularly when used to hide the ugly, leggy, lower stems and branches of some shrubs. Hostas' dense growth and thick, shade-providing leaves allow them to suppress weeds.

## Recommended

Hostas have been subjected to a great deal of crossbreeding and hybridizing, resulting in hundreds of cultivars. Some popular cultivars are **'Francee,'** with puckered, dark green leaves and narrow, white edges; **'Elegans,'** with deeply puckered, blue-grey foliage; **'Frances Williams,'** with puckered, blue-green leaves and yellow-green edges; **'Sum & Substance,'** with immense, green-gold leaves; and **'August Moon,'** with large, slightly puckered, yellow leaves.

---

**Features:** decorative foliage; white or purple, summer and fall flowers **Height:** 10–90 cm (4–36") **Spread:** 15 cm–1.8 m (6"–6') **Hardiness:** zones 3–8

# Iris

*Iris*

Irises are steeped in history and lore. Iris flowers come in all the colours of the rainbow, and the name *Iris* is from the Greek word meaning "rainbow."

## Growing

Irises prefer **full sun** but tolerate very light or dappled shade. The soil should be of **average fertility** and **well drained**. Japanese irises and Siberian irises prefer a moist, well-drained soil. Divide in late summer or early fall. Deadhead irises to keep them tidy. Cut back the foliage of Siberian irises in spring.

## Tips

All irises are popular border plants, but Japanese irises and Siberian irises are also useful alongside streams or ponds. Dwarf cultivars make attractive additions to rock gardens.

## Recommended

Many species and hybrids are available. Among the most popular is the bearded iris, often a hybrid of **I. germanica**. It has the widest range of flower colours but is susceptible to attack from the iris borer, which can kill a plant. Several irises are not susceptible, including Japanese iris (**I. ensata**) and Siberian iris (**I. sibirica**). Check with your local garden centre to find out what's available.

*I. sibirica* (above), *I. germanica* 'Stepping Out' (below)

*Wash your hands after handling irises; they can cause severe internal irritation if ingested.*

**Features:** spring, summer and sometimes fall flowers in many shades of pink, red, purple, blue, white, brown or yellow; attractive foliage **Height:** 10 cm–1.2 m (4"–4') **Spread:** 15 cm–1.2 m (6"–4') **Hardiness:** zones 3–8

# Lungwort
*Pulmonaria*

*P. saccharata* (above & below)

Lungworts have highly attractive foliage that ranges in colour from apple green to silver-spotted and olive to dark emerald.

## Growing

Lungworts prefer **partial to full shade**. The soil should be **fertile, humus rich, moist** and **well drained**. Rot can occur in very wet soil.

Divide in early summer after flowering or in fall. Provide the newly planted

divisions with lots of water to help them re-establish.

## Tips

Lungworts make useful and attractive groundcovers for shady borders, woodland gardens and pond and stream edges.

## Recommended

*P. longifolia* (long-leaved lungwort) forms a dense clump of long, narrow, white-spotted, green leaves and bears clusters of blue flowers.

*P. saccharata* (Bethlehem sage) forms a compact clump of large, white-spotted, evergreen leaves and pink-budded flowers that turn blue as they mature. Many cultivars are available.

**Features:** decorative, mottled foliage; blue, red, pink or white, spring flowers
**Height:** 20–60 cm (8–24")
**Spread:** 20–90 cm (8–36")
**Hardiness:** zones 3–8

# Lupine
### *Lupinus*

Spikes of brightly coloured flowers create a splendid riot of colour when lupines are planted in groups in a border.

## Growing

Lupines grow well in **full sun** and **partial shade** in a location sheltered from strong winds. The soil should be **average to fertile, sandy, slightly acidic** and **well drained**. Plants don't need dividing and resent having their roots disturbed. The small offsets that form at the bases can be transplanted when young, as can the seedlings that are bound to sprout up around the plants. Deadheading keeps plants looking tidy but reduces the likelihood of self-seeding.

## Tips

Lupines are lovely when massed together in beds, borders and cottage-style gardens and when naturalized in meadow plantings.

## Recommended

*L.* **Russell Hybrids** were developed from the cross-breeding of several species of lupine. The result is compact plants that bear flowers in a wide range of colours. The spring and early-summer flowers are produced in a wide range of solid colours and bicolours, though blue tends to dominate in self-seeded offspring. Occasionally, a stunning, luminous purple or pink flower may appear as a pleasant surprise.

*L.* Russell Hybrids (above & below)

*Lupines are in the same plant family as beans and peas, but their pods and seeds are toxic.*

**Features:** white, cream, pink, yellow, blue or purple, often bicoloured, spring and early-summer flowers; attractive, slightly fuzzy foliage **Height:** 60–90 cm (24–36") **Spread:** 30–45 cm (12–18") **Hardiness:** zones 3–8

# Marsh Marigold

*Caltha*

*C. palustris* (above & below)

Marsh marigolds are harbingers of spring, offering glossy, green leaves and bright yellow flowers when most other plants have barely started to sprout.

## Growing

Marsh marigolds grow well in **full sun** and **partial shade**. The soil should be of **average fertility** and **moist**. These plants tolerate wet or periodically flooded soil, often growing next to or in streams, ponds and lakes. Plants often die back and go dormant in summer. Divide every two or three years, after flowering has finished in spring.

## Tips

Marsh marigolds are beautiful, native plants that make an excellent addition to areas of the garden that stay damp or wet. When grown in borders they should be kept well watered. Plant them together with plants that are slow to start in spring but will fill in the space left as marsh marigolds become dormant in mid-summer.

## Recommended

*C. palustris* forms a low mound of glossy, heart-shaped leaves. Yellow flowers are produced in spring. Cultivars with double flowers or white flowers are also available.

**Features:** yellow or white, spring flowers; attractive foliage  **Height:** 20–40 cm (8–16")
**Spread:** 25–50 cm (10–20")
**Hardiness:** zones 2–8

# Meadowsweet

*Filipendula*

For an impressive, informal, vertical accent and showy clusters of fluffy, fragrant flowers, meadowsweet is second to none.

## Growing

Meadowsweet prefers **partial shade** or **light shade** but tolerates full sun if the soil remains sufficiently moist. The soil should be **fertile, deep, humus rich** and **moist**, except in the case of *F. vulgaris*, which prefers dry soil. Divide in spring or fall.

## Tips

Meadowsweet is excellent for bog gardens or wet sites. Grow it alongside streams or in moist meadows. Meadowsweet may also be grown in the back of a border, as long as it is kept well watered. Grow *F. vulgaris* if you can't provide the moisture needed by the other species.

## Recommended

*F. rubra* (queen-of-the-prairie) forms a large, spreading clump and bears clusters of fragrant, pink flowers. Cultivars are available.

*F. vulgaris* (dropwort, meadowsweet) is a low-growing species that bears clusters of fragrant, creamy white flowers. Cultivars with double or pink flowers or variegated foliage are available.

*F. rubra* (below)

*Deadhead meadowsweet if you so desire, but the faded seedheads are quite attractive when left in place.*

**Features:** white, cream, pink or red, late-spring or summer flowers; attractive foliage **Height:** 60 cm–2.4 m (2–8') **Spread:** 45 cm–1.2 m (18"–4') **Hardiness:** zones 3–8

# Monkshood

*Aconitum*

These elegant plants add a cooling and contrasting touch of blue to the garden late in the season when oranges and yellows seem to dominate the scene.

## Growing

Moonkshoods grow best in **light shade** or **partial shade**. Any **moist** soil will do, but a **fertile, humus rich** soil is preferred. Mulch plants to keep roots cool and moist. Divide plants in late fall or early spring only for propagation, as they resent having their roots disturbed and are slow to re-establish. Don't plant too deeply or the crown may rot.

Tall monkshoods may need staking. Use twigs or peony hoops, and plants will fill in and hide the supports.

## Tips

Monkshood plants are perfect for cool, boggy locations along streams or next to ponds. They make tall, elegant additions to woodland gardens in combination with lower-growing plants.

## Recommended

*A. x cammarum* (Cammarum hybrids) includes several of the most popular of the hybrids. **'Bicolor'** (bicolor monkshood) bears blue and white, helmet-shaped flowers. **'Bressingham Spire'** bears spikes of dark purple-blue flowers on strong plants that need no staking.

*A. napellus* (common monkshood) is an upright plant that forms a basal mound of finely divided foliage. It bears dark purple-blue flowers.

*A. x cammarum* 'Bicolor' (above), *A. napellus* (below)

Also called: wolfsbane Features: blue, purple or white, late-summer and early-fall flowers; attractive foliage Height: 90 cm–1.8 m (3–6') Spread: 30–45 cm (12–18") Hardiness: zones 3–8

# Peony

*Paeonia*

From the simple, single flowers to the extravagant doubles, it's easy to become mesmerized by these voluptuous plants. Once the fleeting, but magnificent, flower display is done, the foliage remains stellar throughout the growing season.

### Growing

Peonies prefer **full sun** but tolerate some shade. The planting site should be well prepared before the plants are introduced. Peonies like **fertile, humus-rich, moist, well-drained** soil to which lots of compost has been added. Mulch peonies lightly with compost in spring. Too much fertilizer, particularly nitrogen, causes floppy growth and reduces blooming. Division is not required but can be done in fall to propagate plants. Deadhead to keep plants looking tidy.

### Tips

These wonderful plants look great in a border combined with other early bloomers. They may be underplanted with bulbs and other plants that will die down by mid-summer, when the emerging foliage of peonies will hide the dying foliage of spring plants. Avoid planting peonies under trees, where they will have to compete for moisture and nutrients.

Planting depth determines whether or not a peony will flower. Tubers planted too shallow or, more commonly, too deep will not flower. The buds or eyes on the tuber should be 2.5–5 cm (1–2") below the soil surface.

*P. lactiflora* 'Shimmering Velvet' (above)
*P. lactiflora* cultivars (below)

Place peony cages around the plants in early spring to support the heavy flowers. The foliage will grow up into the wires and hide the cage.

### Recommended

There are hundreds of peonies available. Cultivars come in a wide range of colours, may have single or double flowers and may or may not be fragrant. Visit your local garden centre to see what is available.

**Features:** white, cream, yellow, pink, red or purple, spring and early-summer flowers; attractive foliage **Height:** 60–80 cm (24–32") **Spread:** 60–80 cm (24–32") **Hardiness:** zones 2–8

# Phlox

*Phlox*

P. subulata (above), P. paniculata (below)

Phlox comes in many shapes and sizes, from low creepers to tall, bushy border plants. Its fragrant flowers come in a range of colours with blooming times from early spring to mid-fall.

## Growing

*P. paniculata* and *P. maculata* prefer **full sun**. *P. subulata* prefers **full sun to partial shade**. All like **fertile, humus-rich, moist, well-drained** soil. Divide in fall or spring.

## Tips

Low-growing species look good in rock gardens, at the front of borders or cascading over retaining walls. Taller phloxes may be used in the middle of borders and are particularly effective planted in groups.

## Recommended

**P. maculata** (meadow phlox, wild sweet William) forms an upright clump of hairy stems with narrow leaves that are sometimes spotted with red. Pink, purple or white, early-summer flowers are borne in conical clusters.

**P. paniculata** (garden phlox, summer phlox) is a tall, upright, summer- and fall-blooming plant with many cultivars in various sizes and flower colours. Look for powdery mildew-resistant cultivars like **'David,'** a beautiful, white-flowered cultivar.

**P. subulata** (moss phlox, moss pink) is very low growing. Its flowers come in various colours and blanket the evergreen foliage. A light shearing after the plant finishes flowering in June will encourage tidy growth and occasionally a second flush of flowers.

*Unfortunately, garden phlox is a favourite of deer. Weekly applications of Plantskydd®, a blood-based deer repellent, can protect it.*

**Features:** white, blue, purple, orange, pink or red, spring, summer or fall flowers **Height:** 5 cm–1.2 m (2"–4') **Spread:** 30–90 cm (12–36") **Hardiness:** zones 3–8

# Pinks
## *Dianthus*

*D. gratianopolitanus* 'Bath's Pink' (above), *D. plumarius* (below)

From tiny and delicate to large and robust, this genus contains a wide variety of plants, many with spice-scented flowers.

## Growing

Pinks prefer **full sun** but tolerate some light shade. A **well-drained, neutral to alkaline** soil is required. The most important factor in the successful cultivation of pinks is drainage—they hate to stand in water. Rocky outcroppings make up the native habitat of many species.

## Tips

Pinks make excellent plants for rock gardens and rock walls and for edging flower borders and walkways. They can also be used in cutting gardens and even as groundcovers. To prolong blooming, deadhead as the flowers fade, but leave a few flowers in place to go to seed.

## Recommended

*D. deltoides* (maiden pink) forms a mat of foliage and flowers in shades of red and pink.

*D. gratianopolitanus* (cheddar pink) is long lived and forms a very dense mat of evergreen, silver-grey foliage with sweet-scented flowers, mostly in shades of pink.

*D. plumarius* (cottage pink) is noteworthy for its role in the development of many popular cultivars known collectively as garden pinks. The flowers can be single, semi-double or fully double and are available in many colours.

**Features:** sometimes-fragrant, pink, red, white or purple, spring or summer flowers; attractive foliage **Height:** 5–45 cm (2–18") **Spread:** 15–30 cm (6–12") **Hardiness:** zones 3–8

# Plume Poppy

*Macleaya*

*M. cordata* (above & below)

*P*lume poppy is bold, not only in its visual presence, but also in its space-grabbing maneuvers.

## Growing

Plume poppy prefers **full sun** but tolerates partial shade. The soil should be of **average fertility, humus rich** and **moist**. Plume poppy tolerates dry soils and is less invasive in poorer conditions. Divide every two or three years in spring or fall to control the size of the clump.

Pull up or cut back any overly exuberant growth as needed. Planting in a heavy-duty, bottomless container sunk into the ground will slow invasive spreading.

## Tips

Plume poppy makes an impressive specimen plant and looks good at the back of a border. It quickly creates a summer screen and makes a good choice for the centre of a cement-bordered median or large island bed.

## Recommended

*M. cordata* is a tall, narrow, clump-forming plant with impressive, dinner-plate sized, deeply lobed leaves and plumes of creamy white flowers.

*Deadhead if you do not want self-sown seedlings popping up all over.*

**Features:** cream-coloured, mid- to late-summer flowers; attractive foliage; shrub-like habit **Height:** 1.8–3 m (6–10') **Spread:** 30–90 cm (12–36") **Hardiness:** zones 3–8

# Purple Coneflower

*Echinacea*

Purple coneflower is a visual delight, with its mauve petals offset by a spiky, orange centre.

## Growing

Purple coneflower grows well in **full sun** or very **light shade**. It tolerates any **well-drained** soil but prefers an **average to rich** soil. The thick taproots make this plant drought resistant, but it prefers to have regular water. Divide every four years or so in spring or fall.

Deadhead early in the flowering season to prolong blooming. Later you may wish to leave the flowerheads in place to self-seed and to provide winter interest. Pinch plants back or thin out the stems in early summer to encourage bushy growth that is less prone to mildew.

## Tips

Use purple coneflower in meadow gardens and informal borders, either in groups or as single specimens.

The dry flowerheads make an interesting feature in fall and winter gardens.

## Recommended

*E. purpurea* is an upright plant covered in prickly hairs. It bears long-lasting, purple flowers with orange centres and attractive, droopy petals. Cultivars are available, including several popular new varieties with yellow or orange flowers.

*E. purpurea* 'Magnus' and 'White Swan' (above)
*E. purpurea* (below)

*Purple coneflower attracts wildlife to the garden, providing pollen, nectar and seeds to various hungry visitors.*

**Also called:** coneflower, echinacea
**Features:** purple, pink, white, yellow or orange, mid-summer to fall flowers with rusty orange centres; persistent seedheads
**Height:** 60 cm–1.8 m (2–6') **Spread:** 30–60 cm (12–24") **Hardiness:** zones 3–8

# Rockcress

*Arabis/Aubrieta*

These lovely spring bloomers share a common name as well as a low-growing, cascading habit; they are both perfect additions to rock gardens and walls.

## Growing

Both species prefer **full sun** but *Aubrieta* will tolerate partial shade. The soil should be of **average fertility, neutral to slightly alkaline, moist** and **well drained**. Divide every three or so years to keep plants from thinning out in the middle. Plants can be cut back by up to half once they are finished blooming to keep them neat and compact and to promote new growth and an occasional second flush of blooms.

## Tips

Use rockcress in rock gardens, to edge borders, on rock walls, between the paving stones of a pathway or as groundcovers on difficult-to-mow slopes. Avoid planting them where they may overwhelm slower-growing plants.

## Recommended

*Arabis alpina* subsp. *caucasica* (*A. caucasica*) forms a low mound of small rosettes of foliage. It bears white flowers, though at least one pink-flowered cultivar is available.

*Aubrieta deltoidea* is a low, mound-forming plant that bears pink, purple or white flowers. Cultivars and hybrids are available.

*Arabis alpina* subsp. *caucasica* (above)
*Aubrieta deltoidea* 'Bowles Purple' (below)

*Arabis is one of the first perennials to bloom in Maritime gardens as the early bulbs like crocus and snowdrops fade away.*

**Features:** white, pink or purple, spring flowers; attractive foliage and habit **Height:** 5–30 cm (2–12") **Spread:** 30–60 cm (12–24") **Hardiness:** zones 4–8

# Russian Sage

*Perovskia*

*P. atriplicifolia* (above), *P. atriplicifolia* 'Filigran' (below)

Russian sage offers four-season interest in the garden: soft, grey-green leaves on light grey stems in spring; fuzzy, violet-blue flowers in summer; and silvery white stems in fall that last until late winter.

## Growing

Russian sage prefers **full sun**. The soil should be **poor to moderately fertile** and **well drained**. Too much water and nitrogen will cause this plant's growth to flop, so do not plant it next to heavy feeders. Russian sage cannot be divided because it is a subshrub that grows from a single stem.

In spring, when new growth appears low on the branches, or in fall, cut the plant back hard to about 15–30 cm (6–12") to encourage vigorous, bushy growth.

## Tips

The silvery foliage and blue flowers work well with other plants in the back of a mixed border and soften the appearance of daylilies. Russian sage can also create a soft screen in a natural garden or on a dry bank. A raised, well-drained bed is key to survival through our soggy Maritime winters.

## Recommended

*P. atriplicifolia* is a loose, upright plant with silvery white, finely divided foliage. The small, lavender blue flowers are loosely held on silvery, branched stems. Cultivars are available.

*Russian sage blossoms make a lovely addition to fresh bouquets and dried-flower arrangements.*

**Features:** blue or purple, mid-summer to fall flowers; attractive habit; fragrant, grey-green foliage **Height:** 90 cm–1.2 m (3–4')
**Spread:** 90 cm–1.2 m (3–4')
**Hardiness:** zones 4–8

# Saxifrage

*Saxifraga*

S. *arendsii* cultivar (above & below)

Saxifrage is a dense, low-growing plant ideal for crowding out weeds on rocky walls and providing airy sprays of flowers to the early-summer garden.

## Growing

Saxifrage grows best in **partial shade** with afternoon shade being preferred. The soil should be **fertile, neutral to alkaline, moist** and **well drained**. The small rosettes that form at the base of the plants can be removed and replanted to propagate more plants.

## Tips

Saxifrage makes a good addition to lightly shaded rock gardens and walls and can be used as a groundcover and to edge beds and borders.

## Recommended

*S.* x *arendsii* **hybrids** (mossy saxifrage) usually form low mounds of bright green foliage. Late-spring flowers may be red, white, yellow, pink or purple. Several named hybrids are available.

**Features:** pink, white, red, yellow or purple, late-spring or early-summer flowers; dense habit **Height:** 10–20 cm (4–8") **Spread:** 15–30 cm (6–12") **Hardiness:** zones 4–8

# Sea Holly
*Eryngium*

E. alpinum (above & below)

Sea hollies add structure and interest to the garden with their silvery blue flowers, angular growth habit and striking, thistly bracts.

## Growing

Sea hollies grow best in **full sun**. The soil should be **average to fertile** and **well drained**. These plants have a long taproot and are fairly drought tolerant, though they grow best if not left dry for too long. They are tolerant of seaside conditions. Avoid dividing them because they resent having their roots disturbed.

## Tips

Mix sea hollies with other late-season bloomers in a border. They make an interesting addition to naturalized gardens.

Wear gloves when handling these plants as the leaves and flower bracts are spiny.

## Recommended

*E. alpinum* (alpine sea holly) grows 60 cm–1.2 m (2–4') tall and bears steel blue or white flowers. Cultivars are available.

**Features:** attractive stems, foliage and flowers **Height:** 30 cm–1.5 m (1–5') **Spread:** 30–60 cm (12–24") **Hardiness:** zones 4–8

# Sedum

*Sedum*

S. *acre* (above), S. 'Autumn Joy' (below)

Some 300 to 500 species of sedum are distributed throughout the northern hemisphere. Many sedums are grown for their foliage, which can range in colour from steel grey-blue and green to red and burgundy.

## Growing

Sedums prefer **full sun** but tolerate partial shade. The soil should be of **average fertility, very well drained** and **neutral to alkaline**. Divide in spring when needed.

## Tips

Low-growing sedums make wonderful groundcovers and additions to rock gardens or rock walls. They also edge beds and borders beautifully. Taller sedums make a lovely late-season display in a bed or border.

## Recommended

*S. acre* (gold moss stonecrop) is a low-growing, wide-spreading plant that bears small, yellow-green flowers. It can spread aggressively.

*S. 'Autumn Joy'* (autumn joy sedum) is a popular upright hybrid. The flowers open pink or red and later fade to deep bronze. It is one of the longest-blooming perennials.

*Early-summer pruning of upright species and hybrids encourages compact, bushy growth but can delay flowering.*

**Also called:** stonecrop **Features:** yellow, white, red or pink, summer to fall flowers; decorative, fleshy foliage **Height:** 5–60 cm (2–24") **Spread:** 30–60 cm (12–24") or more **Hardiness:** zones 3–8

# Sneezeweed

*Helenium*

These daisy-like flowers, with their plump, raised, sometimes contrasting centres, add a delightful charm to the late-summer and fall garden.

### Growing

Sneezeweed grows best in **full sun**. The soil should be **fertile, moist** and **well drained**. Be sure to water well during summer dry spells to prevent plants from dropping their lower leaves. Dead-head to prolong blooming. Divide when clumps start to become overgrown and begin to thin in the middle.

### Tips

Sneezeweed adds bright colour to the border in late summer and fall. It looks at home in an informal cottage or meadow garden. It will also work well in the moist soil near a pond or other water feature where it will get regular water. Sneezeweed makes an excellent addition to fresh bouquets.

### Recommended

*H. autumnale* forms an upright clump of stems and narrow foliage. It bears yellow, red, bronze, orange, maroon or bicoloured, daisy-like flowers in late summer and fall. Many cultivars are available and often have more compact habits.

*H. autumnale* (above & below)

*Sneezeweed was formerly used as a substitute for snuff.*

**Also called:** Helen's flower **Features:** red, orange, yellow, maroon, brown or bicoloured, late-summer and fall flowers; attractive habit **Height:** 75 cm–1.8 m (30"–6') **Spread:** 45–90 cm (18–36") **Hardiness:** zones 3–8

# Snow-in-Summer

*Cerastium*

*C. tomentosum* (above & below)

This lovely plant has a delicate appearance that belies its tough-as-nails nature. It thrives in even the most neglected and difficult conditions.

## Growing

Snow-in-summer grows well in **full sun** and **partial shade**. **Well-drained** soil of any type is suitable. Wet soil may cause root rot, and overly rich soil promotes rampant spread. Divide when the plant begins to thin out in the centre. Trim it back after flowering to keep it looking tidy and to somewhat control its spread.

## Tips

Snow-in-summer is well suited to sunny, hot locations and makes a good ground-cover under shrubs and taller plants. It can be used to edge borders and is particularly useful when the border edges a paved drive or walkway, where plants that are less heat tolerant may not do as well. It can also be used to prevent erosion on banks that are too steep to mow.

## Recommended

*C. tomentosum* forms a low mat of silvery grey foliage and bears white flowers in late spring.

*Snow-in-summer is one of the best perennials for cascading over a retaining wall.*

**Features:** white, late-spring flowers; spreading habit **Height:** 5–20 cm (2–8") **Spread:** indefinite **Hardiness:** zones 1–8

# Thrift

## *Armeria*

These tough plants form cushion-like mounds from which lollipop-like flowers emerge.

### Growing

Thrift grows best in **full sun**. The soil should be of **poor to average fertility, sandy** and **well drained**. Thrift is drought tolerant once established. Prompt deadheading prolongs the flowering period. Excess fertilizer will reduce flowering and can eventually kill the plant.

### Tips

Thrift is a useful plant for rock gardens or the front of a border. It is tolerant of seaside conditions and will grow well in coastal gardens. Cut plants back if they seem to be thinning in the middle to encourage new growth.

### Recommended

*A. maritima* forms a clump of grassy foliage. Ball-like clusters of pink, white or purple flowers are borne at the ends of long stems in late spring and early summer. The plant grows up to 20 cm (8") tall. Cultivars are available, including **'Alba,'** with white flowers, and **'Rubrifolia,'** with burgundy leaves.

*A. maritima* (above & below)

*It has been suggested that this plant is called thrift because it has one root supporting many stalks, so it is "thrifty" with its roots.*

**Also called:** sea pink, sea thrift
**Features:** pink, white, red or purple, late-spring and summer flowers; clump-forming habit; grass-like foliage **Height:** 20–60 cm (8–24") **Spread:** 30–60 cm (12–24")
**Hardiness:** zones 3–8

# Yarrow

*Achillea*

A. millefolium 'Paprika' (above), A. filipendulina (below)

*Yarrows make excellent groundcovers. They send up shoots and flowers from a low basal point and may be mowed periodically without excessive damage to the plant. Mower blades should be kept at least 10 cm (4") high.*

Yarrows are informal, tough plants with a fantastic colour range.

## Growing

Yarrows grow best in **full sun**. The soil should be of **average fertility, sandy** and **well drained**. These plants tolerate drought and poor soil. They will also tolerate heavy, wet soil and humidity, but they do not thrive in such conditions. Very rich soil or too much nitrogen fertilizer results in weak, floppy growth. Divide every two or three years in spring.

Deadhead to prolong blooming. Basal foliage should be left in place over the winter and tidied up in spring.

## Tips

Cottage gardens, wildflower gardens and mixed borders are perfect places for these informal plants. They thrive in hot, dry locations where nothing else will grow.

## Recommended

*A. filipendulina* forms a clump of fern-like foliage and bears yellow flowers. It has been used to develop several hybrids and cultivars.

*A. millefolium* (common yarrow) forms a clump of soft, finely divided foliage and bears white flowers. Many cultivars exist, with flowers in a wide range of colours.

**Features:** white, yellow, red, orange, pink or purple, mid-summer to early-fall flowers; attractive foliage; spreading habit **Height:** 10 cm–1.2 m (4"–4') **Spread:** 30–90 cm (12–36") **Hardiness:** zones 3–8

# Bearberry
*Arctostaphylos*

*A. uva-ursi* (above), *A. uva-ursi* cultivar (below)

earberry forms an attractive, low-growing mat of evergreen foliage. The tiny flowers and bright red fruit provide a lovely contrast to the dark green of the leaves.

### Growing
Bearberry grows well in **full sun** and **partial shade**. The soil should be of **poor to average fertility, well drained, acidic** and **moist**, though bearberry will adapt to alkaline soils.

### Tips
Once established, bearberry is a vigorous, wide-spreading groundcover. It makes a good addition to rock gardens and mixed beds and borders. It can be grown on difficult-to-mow slopes as an alternative to grass. Mulch will keep the weeds down until bearberry establishes and fills in.

### Recommended
*A. uva-ursi* is a low-growing, spreading, evergreen plant. It bears white to pink flowers in late spring followed by berries that ripen to bright red. Cultivars are available.

**Also called:** kinnikinnick **Features:** evergreen foliage; white or pink flowers; bright red fruit; mat-forming habit **Height:** 10–15 cm (4–6") **Spread:** 45–90 cm (18–36") **Hardiness:** zones 2–7

# Beech

*Fagus*

F. grandifolia (above), F. sylvatica (below)

*The nuts of the beech tree are
edible when roasted.*

Majestic beeches are attractive at any age, from their big, bold, beautiful youth through to their slow, craggy decline.

### Growing

Beeches grow well in **full sun** or **partial shade**. The soil should be of **average fertility, loamy** and **well drained**, though most well-drained soils are tolerated.

American beech doesn't like having its roots disturbed and should be transplanted only when very young. European beech transplants easily and is more tolerant of varied soil conditions than American beech.

### Tips

Beeches make excellent specimens. They are also used as shade trees and in woodland gardens. These trees need a lot of space, but European beech's adaptability to pruning makes it a reasonable choice in a small garden if you are willing and able to prune it.

### Recommended

*F. grandifolia* (American beech) is a broad-canopied tree native to most of eastern North America.

*F. sylvatica* (European beech) is a spectacular, broad tree with a number of interesting cultivars. Several are small enough to use in the home garden. There are narrow columnar or weeping varieties and varieties with purple foliage, yellow foliage or pink, white and green variegated foliage.

**Features:** large, oval, deciduous shade tree; attractive foliage; smooth, grey bark; fall colour; fruit **Height:** 9–24 m (30–80') **Spread:** 3–20 m (10–65') **Hardiness:** zones 4–8

# Boxwood

*Buxus*

oxwood is now my favourite foundation/garden evergreen, given its full deer resistance, shiny, dense foliage, insect and disease resistance, winter hardiness, shade tolerance and slow growth rate (which keeps it in proportion longer without much pruning).

## Growing

Boxwoods prefer **partial shade** but adapt to full sun if watered regularly. The soil should be **fertile** and **well drained**. Once established, these plants are drought tolerant. A good, rich mulch benefits these shrubs because their roots grow very close to the surface. Try not to disturb the soil around established boxwoods because the roots are easily damaged.

## Tips

Boxwoods make excellent background plants in a mixed border. Brightly coloured plants show up well against the even, dark green surface of boxwoods. Dwarf cultivars can be trimmed into small hedges for edging beds or walkways. An interesting topiary piece can create a formal or whimsical focal point in any garden.

## Recommended

Some of the best boxwood selections are cultivars developed from crosses between *B. microphylla* **var.** *koreana* (Korean boxwood) and *B. sempervirens* (common boxwood). These hybrids combine the cold hardiness and pest resistance of Korean boxwood with the vigour and attractive winter colour of common

*B.* 'Green Mountain' (above & below)

boxwood. **'Green Mountain'** is an upright plant with a pyramidal to oval habit. It grows about 1.5 m (5') tall and spreads up to 1 m (40"). **'Green Velvet'** has a more rounded habit and grows 60–90 cm (24–36") tall with an equal spread.

*Boxwood foliage contains toxic compounds that, when ingested, can cause severe digestive upset.*

**Features:** dense, evergreen shrub with attractive foliage **Height:** 60 cm–4.5 m (2–15') **Spread:** 60 cm–4.5 m (2–15') **Hardiness:** zones 4–8

# Cedar
*Thuja*

*T. occidentalis* 'Yellow Ribbon' (above)
*T. occidentalis* (below)

*The soft, scale-like leaves of cedars make them appealing plants to screen children's play areas; they won't poke tender skin as many of the needles of evergreens can.*

Cedars are rot resistant, durable and long lived, earning quiet admiration from gardeners everywhere.

## Growing
Cedars prefer **full sun** but tolerate light to partial shade. The soil should be of **average fertility, moist** and **well drained**. Wild cedars are usually located in lime-rich soil, and cultivated trees benefit from an annual addition of lime. These plants enjoy humidity and in the wild are often found growing near marshy areas. Cedars will perform best in a location with some shelter from wind, especially in winter when the foliage can easily dry out and give the entire plant a rather brown, drab appearance.

## Tips
Large varieties of cedars make excellent specimen trees, and smaller cultivars can be used in foundation plantings and shrub borders and as formal or informal hedges. Trim cedar hedges annually in an A-frame shape under 2 m (7') so it can be done without a ladder.

## Recommended
*T. occidentalis* (eastern arborvitae, eastern white cedar) is a narrow, pyramidal tree with scale-like, evergreen needles. There are dozens of cultivars available, including shrubby dwarf varieties, varieties with yellow foliage and smaller, upright varieties. (Zones 2–7; cultivars may be less cold hardy)

**Also called:** arborvitae  **Features:** small to large, evergreen shrub or tree; foliage; bark; form  **Height:** 60 cm–15 m (2–50')  **Spread:** 60 cm–6 m (2–20')  **Hardiness:** zones 2–8

# Crabapple
*Malus*

$\mathcal{P}$ure white through deep pink flowers, heights between 1.5 and 9 m (5–30') with similar spreads, tolerance of winter's extreme cold and summer's baking heat and small, yellow through candy apple red fruit often persisting through winter—choose a cultivar with fungus and disease resistance, and what more could anyone ask from a tree?

## Growing

Crabapples prefer **full sun** but tolerate partial shade. The soil should be of **average to rich fertility, moist** and **well drained**. These trees tolerate damp soil.

One of the best ways to prevent the spread of crabapple pests and diseases is to clean up all the leaves and fruit that fall off the tree. Many pests overwinter in the fruit, leaves or soil at the base of the tree. Clearing away their winter shelter helps keep populations under control.

Keep an eye out for pencil-sized, round holes in the trunk near the ground, a sign of apple borer, which can kill a tree in one to three seasons.

## Tips

Crabapples make excellent specimen plants. Many varieties are quite small, so there is one to suit almost any size of garden. Some forms are even small enough to grow in large containers. Crabapples' flexible, young branches make them good choices for creating espalier specimens along a wall or fence.

## Recommended

There are hundreds of crabapples available. When choosing a species, variety or cultivar, one of the most important attributes to look for is disease resistance. Even the most beautiful flowers, fruit or habit will never look good if the plant is ravaged by pests or diseases. Ask for information about new, resistant cultivars at your local nursery or garden centre.

---

**Features:** rounded, mounded or spreading, small to medium, deciduous tree; spring flowers; late-season and winter fruit; fall foliage; habit; bark **Height:** 1.5–9 m (5–30')
**Spread:** 1.8–9 m (6–30')
**Hardiness:** zones 4–8

# Dogwood
*Cornus*

*C. alba* 'Baihalo' (above), *C. alba* (below)

Whether your garden is wet, dry, sunny or shaded, there is a dogwood for almost every condition. Stem colour, leaf variegation, fall colour, growth habit, soil adaptability and hardiness are all positive attributes to be found in dogwoods.

## Growing
Dogwoods grow equally well in **full sun, light shade** and **partial shade**, with a slight preference for light shade. The soil should be of **average to high fertility, high in organic matter, neutral to slightly acidic** and **well drained**.

## Tips
Shrub dogwoods look best in groups rather than as single specimens. Use them along the edge of a woodland, in a shrub or mixed border, alongside a house or near a pond, water feature or patio.

## Recommended
*C. alba* (red-twig dogwood, Tartarian dogwood) and *C. sericea* (*C. stolonifera*; red-osier dogwood) are grown for their bright red stems that provide winter interest. Fall foliage colour can also be attractive. Cultivars are available with stems in varied shades of red, orange and yellow. *C. alba* '**Elegantissima**' (silverleaf dogwood) has striking, variegated foliage and great shade tolerance.

**Features:** deciduous, large shrub or small tree; late-spring to early-summer flowers; fall foliage; stem colour; fruit  **Height:** 1.5–3 m (5–10')  **Spread:** 1.5–3 m (5–10')  **Hardiness:** zones 2–7

# Elder

*Sambucus*

Elders work well in a naturalized garden. Cultivars are available that will provide light texture in a dark area, dark foliage in a bright area or variegated yellow foliage and bright stems in brilliant sunshine.

## Growing

Elders grow well in **full sun** or **partial shade**. Cultivars and varieties grown for interesting leaf colour develop the best colour in light or partial shade. The soil should be of **average fertility, moist** and **well drained**. These plants tolerate dry soil once established.

## Tips

Elders can be used in a shrub or mixed border, in a natural woodland garden or next to a pond or other water feature. Types with interesting or colourful foliage can be used as specimen plants or focal points in the garden.

## Recommended

***S. nigra*** (European elder/elderberry, black elder/elderberry) is a rounded shrub with white flowers followed by dark purple berries. Cultivars are available with green, yellow, bronze or purple foliage and deeply divided, feathery foliage.

*S. nigra* 'Aureomarginata' (above)
*S. nigra* 'Gerda' (Black Beauty; below)

*The berries are popular for pies and jelly. The raw berries are marginally edible but not palatable and can cause stomach upset, particularly in children. All other parts of elders are toxic.*

*Both the flowers and the fruit can be used to make wine.*

**Also called:** elderberry **Features:** large, bushy, deciduous shrub; early-summer flowers; fruit; foliage **Height:** 1.5–6 m (5–20')
**Spread:** 1.5–6 m (5–20')
**Hardiness:** zones 3–8

# Euonymus

*Euonymus*

*E. fortunei* 'Emerald n' Gold' (above & below)

Two very different species can be grown, each uniquely and equally valuable as ornamental shrubs.

## Growing

Euonymus species prefer **full sun** and tolerate light or partial shade. Soil of **average to rich fertility** is preferable, but any **moist, well-drained** soil will do.

## Tips

*E. alatus* 'Compacta' can be grown in a shrub or mixed border, as a specimen, in a naturalistic garden or as an informal hedge. *E. fortunei* can be grown as a

shrub in a border or as a hedge. It is an excellent substitute for the more demanding boxwood. The trailing habit also makes it useful as a groundcover or climber.

## Recommended

*E. alatus* **'Compacta'** (dwarf burning bush, winged euonymus) is an attractive, open, mounding, deciduous shrub with vivid, red fall foliage. Winter interest is provided by the corky ridges, or wings, that grow on the stems and branches.

*E. fortunei* (wintercreeper euonymus) as a species is rarely grown owing to the wide and attractive variety of cultivars. These can be prostrate, climbing or mounding evergreens, often with attractive, variegated foliage.

**Features:** deciduous or evergreen shrub, groundcover or climber; attractive foliage; fall colour **Height:** 50 cm–6 m (20"–20') **Spread:** 50 cm–6 m (20"–20') **Hardiness:** zones 4–8

# False Cypress
## *Chamaecyparis*

Conifer shoppers are blessed with a marvelous selection of false cypresses that offer colour, size, shape and growth habits not available in most other evergreens.

## Growing

False cypresses prefer **full sun**. The soil should be **fertile, moist, neutral to acidic** and **well drained**. Alkaline soils are tolerated. In shaded areas, growth may be sparse or thin. They have high resistance to deer, compared to cedar, and to juniper blight or other pests and diseases.

## Tips

Tree varieties are used as specimen plants and for hedging. The dwarf and slow-growing cultivars are used in borders and rock gardens and as bonsai. False cypress shrubs can be grown near the house or as evergreen specimens in large containers.

## Recommended

There are several available species of false cypress and many cultivars. The scaly foliage can be in a drooping or strand form or in fan-like or feathery sprays and may be dark green, bright green or yellow. Plant forms vary too, from mounding or rounded to tall and pyramidal to narrow with pendulous branches. Check with your local garden centre or nursery to see what is available.

*The oils in the foliage of false cypresses may be irritating to sensitive skin.*

---

**Features:** narrow, pyramidal, evergreen tree or shrub; cultivars vary; foliage; habit; cones **Height:** 50 cm–45 m (20"–150') **Spread:** 50 cm–24 m (20"–80') **Hardiness:** zones 4–8

*C. pisifera* 'Fillifera Aurea' (above)
*C. nootkatensis* 'Pendula' (below)

# Hemlock

*Tsuga*

*T. canadensis* 'Jeddeloh' (above), *T. canadensis* (below)

Many people would agree that eastern hemlock is one of the most beautiful, graceful evergreen trees in the world. The movement, softness and agility of this tree make it welcome in the landscape.

## Growing

Hemlock generally grows well in any light from **full sun to full shade**. The soil should be **humus rich, moist** and

*With the continued popularity of water gardening, hemlock is in demand for the naturalizing effect that it has on pondscapes.*

**well drained**. Hemlock is drought sensitive and grows best in cool, moist conditions. It is also sensitive to air pollution and suffers salt damage, so keep hemlock away from roadways.

## Tips

This elegant tree, with its delicate needles, is one of the most beautiful evergreens to use as a specimen tree. The smaller cultivars may be included in a shrub or mixed border. Hemlock can be pruned to keep it within bounds or shaped to form a hedge. The many dwarf forms are useful in smaller gardens.

## Recommended

*T. canadensis* (eastern hemlock, Canadian hemlock) is a graceful, narrowly pyramidal tree. Many cultivars are available, including groundcover, pendulous and dwarf forms.

---

**Features:** pyramidal or columnar, evergreen tree or shrub; foliage; habit; cones **Height:** 50 cm–24 m (20"–80') **Spread:** 50 cm–10.5 m (20"–35') **Hardiness:** zones 3–8

# Holly

*Ilex*

ollies vary greatly in shape and size and can be beautiful when planted and treated with full consideration for their needs.

## Growing

These plants prefer **full sun** but tolerate partial shade. The soil should be **average to fertile, humus rich** and **moist**. Hollies perform best in **acidic** soil with a pH of 6.5 to 6.0 or lower. Shelter from winter wind to help prevent evergreen leaves from drying out. Apply a summer mulch to keep the roots cool and moist.

## Tips

Hollies can be used in groups, in woodland gardens and in shrub and mixed borders. They can also be shaped into hedges. Winterberry is good for naturalizing in moist sites in the garden. Blue holly has the classic holly foliage—save pruning until December each year and use the clippings for Christmas decorating.

## Recommended

*I. glabra* (inkberry) is a rounded shrub with glossy, deep green, evergreen foliage and dark purple fruit. Cultivars are available. (Zones 4–8)

*I. x meserveae* (meserve holly, blue holly) is a group of hybrids that originated from crosses between tender English holly (*I. aquifolium*) and hardy hollies like prostrate holly (*I. rugosa*). These dense, evergreen shrubs may be erect, mounding or spreading. (Zones 5–8)

*I. x meserveae* hybrid (above)
*I. x meserveae* 'Blue Girl' (below)

*I. verticillata* (winterberry, winterberry holly) is a deciduous, native species grown for its explosion of red fruit that persists into winter. Many cultivars and hybrids are available.

---

**Features:** erect or spreading, evergreen or deciduous shrub or tree; glossy, sometimes spiny foliage; fruit **Height:** 1–15 m (3–50') **Spread:** 1–12 m (3–40') **Hardiness:** zones 3–8

# Horsechestnut

*Aesculus*

*A. hippocastanum* (above & below)

Horsechestnuts, with their immense, regal bearing, have spectacular, early-summer flowers.

## Growing

Horsechestnuts grow well in **full sun** or **partial shade**. The soil should be **fertile, moist** and **well drained**. These trees dislike excessive drought.

## Tips

Horsechestnuts are used as specimen and shade trees. The roots of horsechestnuts can break up sidewalks and patios if planted too close. Plant nuts 8 cm (3") deep as soon as they fall to grow seedlings.

## Recommended

*A. hippocastanum* (common horsechestnut) is a large, rounded tree that will branch right to the ground if grown in an open setting. The flowers, white with yellow or pink marks, are borne in long spikes.

**Features:** rounded or spreading, deciduous tree; early-summer flowers; foliage; spiny fruit **Height:** 2.4–24 m (8–80') **Spread:** 2.4–20 m (8–65') **Hardiness:** zones 3–7

# Hydrangea
*Hydrangea*

ydrangeas have many attractive qualities including showy, often long-lasting flowers and glossy, green leaves, some of which develop beautiful colours in fall.

## Growing

Hydrangeas grow well in **full sun** or **partial shade**, and some species tolerate full shade. Shade or partial shade will reduce leaf and flower scorch in hotter gardens. The soil should be of **average to high fertility, humus rich, moist** and **well drained**. These plants perform best in cool, moist conditions. They need lots of water.

## Tips

Hydrangeas come in many forms and have many uses in the landscape. They can be included in shrub or mixed borders, used as specimens or informal barriers and planted in groups or containers.

## Recommended

*H. arborescens* (smooth hydrangea) is a rounded shrub that flowers well even in shady conditions. This species is rarely grown in favour of the cultivars that bear large clusters of showy, white blossoms.

*H. paniculata* (panicle hydrangea) is a spreading to upright, large shrub or small tree that bears white flowers from late summer to early fall. **'Grandiflora'** (Peegee hydrangea) is a commonly available cultivar. (Zones 4–8)

*H. aborescens* 'Annabelle' (above)
*H. paniculata* 'Grandiflora' (below)

*Cut stems of mature, pink-tinged Peegee flowers 50 cm (20") long just before first frost and dry them as bouquets in vases indoors—they last for years.*

**Features:** mounding or spreading, deciduous shrub or tree; flowers; habit; foliage; bark
**Height:** 1–6 m (3–20') **Spread:** 1–3 m (3–10') **Hardiness:** zones 3–8

# Lilac
## *Syringa*

S. *meyeri* (above), S. *vulgaris* (below)

*Lilacs are known for fragrance, and the dwarf Korean lilac ranks as one of the most fragrant of all ornamental shrubs.*

The hardest thing about growing lilacs is choosing from the many species and hundreds of cultivars available.

### Growing
Lilacs grow best in **full sun**. The soil should be **fertile, humus rich** and **well drained**. These plants tolerate open, windy locations.

### Tips
Include lilacs in a shrub or mixed border or use them to create an informal hedge. Japanese tree lilac can be used as a specimen tree.

### Recommended
**S. *meyeri*** (dwarf Korean lilac, Meyer lilac) is a compact, rounded shrub that bears fragrant, pink or lavender flowers. (Zones 3–7)

**S. *reticulata*** (Japanese tree lilac) is a rounded, large shrub or small tree that bears fragrant, white flowers. **'Ivory Silk'** has a more compact habit and produces more flowers than the species. (Zones 3–7)

**S. *vulgaris*** (French lilac, common lilac) is the plant most people think of when they think of lilacs. It is a suckering, spreading shrub with an irregular habit that bears fragrant, lilac-coloured flowers. Hundreds of cultivars with a variety of flower colours are available. (Zones 3–8)

**Features:** rounded or suckering, deciduous shrub or small tree; late-spring to mid-summer flowers; habit **Height:** 1–9 m (3–30')
**Spread:** 1–7.5 m (3–25')
**Hardiness:** zones 2–8

# Linden

## *Tilia*

Lindens are picturesque shade trees with a signature pyramidal form and sweet-scented flowers that capture the essence of summer.

### Growing

Lindens grow best in **full sun**. The soil should be **average to fertile, moist** and **well drained**. These trees adapt to most pH levels but prefer an alkaline soil. They tolerate pollution and urban conditions.

### Tips

Lindens are useful and attractive street trees, shade trees and specimen trees. Their tolerance of pollution and their neat, oval form make lindens ideal for city gardens.

### Recommended

*T. cordata* (littleleaf linden) is a dense, pyramidal tree that may become rounded with age. It bears small, fragrant flowers with narrow, yellow-green bracts. Cultivars are available.

*T. cordata* (above)

*Open-grown lindens tend to branch right to the ground. Lower branches can be removed annually if you don't want the tree in your home lawn to do this.*

**Features:** dense, pyramidal to rounded, deciduous tree; habit; foliage **Height:** 6–20 m (20–65') **Spread:** 4.5–15 m (15–50') **Hardiness:** zones 3–8

# Maple
*Acer*

*A. ginnala* 'Bailey Compact' (above)
*A. palmatum* cultivar (below)

*Maple wood is hard and dense and is used for fine furniture construction, flooring and some musical instruments.*

Maples are attractive all year, with delicate flowers in spring, attractive foliage and hanging samaras in summer, vibrant leaf colour in fall and interesting bark and branch structures in winter.

## Growing

Generally maples do well in **full sun** or **light shade**, though this varies from species to species. The soil should be **fertile, moist, humus rich** and **well drained**.

## Tips

Maples can be used as specimen trees, as large elements in shrub or mixed borders or as hedges. Some are useful as understory plants bordering wooded areas; others can be grown in containers on patios or terraces. Japanese maple is the quintessential Japanese garden tree. Small-leaved varieties, such as amur and Japanese maple, are well suited to creating bonsai.

## Recommended

Maples are some of the most popular shade or street trees. Many are very large when fully mature, but there are also a few smaller species that are useful in smaller gardens, including *A. ginnala* (amur maple; zones 2–8) and *A. palmatum* (Japanese maple; zones 5–8). Check with your local nursery or garden centre for availability.

**Features:** small, multi-stemmed, deciduous tree or large shrub; foliage; bark; winged fruit; fall colour; form; flowers **Height:** 1.8–24 m (6–80') **Spread:** 1.8–21 m (6–70') **Hardiness:** zones 2–8

# Ninebark

*Physocarpus*

P. opulifolius DIABOLO (above & below)

his attractive native deserves wider recognition, especially now that cultivars, with foliage ranging in colour from yellow to purple, are available.

## Growing

Ninebark grows well in **full sun** or **partial shade**. The best leaf colouring develops in a sunny location. The soil should be **fertile, acidic, moist** and **well drained**.

## Tips

Ninebark can be included in a shrub or mixed border, in a woodland garden or in a naturalistic garden. DIABOLO is a healthier substitute for purpleleaf sand cherry as a fast-growing, purple-leafed, upright shrub 2.4 m (8') tall or more.

## Recommended

*P. opulifolius* is a suckering shrub with long, arching branches and exfoliating bark. It bears light pink flowers in early summer and fruit that ripens to reddish green in fall. Recommended cultivars include **'Dart's Gold,'** DIABOLO and SUMMER WINE.

**Also called:** common ninebark
**Features:** upright, sometimes suckering, deciduous shrub; early-summer flowers; fruit; bark; foliage **Height:** 1.2–3 m (4–10')
**Spread:** 1.2–4.5 m (4–15')
**Hardiness:** zones 2–8

# Oak

*Quercus*

The oak's classic shape, outstanding fall colour, deep roots and long life are some of its many assets. Plant it for its individual beauty and for posterity.

### Growing
Oak grows well in **full sun** or **partial shade**. The soil should be **fertile, moist** and **well drained**. This tree can be difficult to establish; transplant it only while it is young.

### Tips
The oak is a large tree that is best as a specimen or for groves in parks and large gardens. Do not disturb the ground around the base of an oak; this tree is very sensitive to changes in grade.

### Recommended
There are many oaks to choose from. A couple of popular species are **Q. robur** (English oak), a rounded, spreading tree with golden yellow fall colour; and **Q. rubra** (red oak), a rounded, spreading tree with fall colour ranging from yellow to red-brown. Some cultivars are available. Check with your local nursery or garden centre.

*Q. robur* (above & below)

*Acorns are generally not edible, though acorns of certain oak species are edible but usually must be processed first to leach out the bitter tannins.*

**Features:** large, rounded, spreading, deciduous tree; summer and fall foliage; bark; habit; acorns **Height:** 10–30 m (33–100') **Spread:** 3–30 m (10–100') **Hardiness:** zones 3–8

# Pine

*Pinus*

Pines offer exciting possibilities for any garden. Exotic-looking pines are available with soft or stiff needles, needles with yellow bands, trunks with patterned or mother-of-pearl-like bark and varied forms.

## Growing

Pines grow best in **full sun**. These trees adapt to most **well-drained** soils but do not tolerate polluted urban conditions.

## Tips

Pines can be used as specimen trees, as hedges or to create windbreaks. Smaller cultivars can be included in shrub or mixed borders. These trees are not heavy feeders; fertilizing will encourage rapid new growth that is weak and susceptible to pest and disease problems.

## Recommended

There are many available pines, both trees and shrubby dwarf plants. Several popular species include *P. aristata* (bristlecone pine), *P. nigra* (Austrian pine), *P. strobus* (white pine) and *P. mugo* **'Pumilio'** (dwarf mugo pine). Check with your local garden centre or nursery to find out what is available.

*Most pines' seeds are edible, though many are too small to bother with. Commercially available "pine nuts" come from* P. pinea *and a few other species.*

P. aristata (above), P. strobus (below)

---

**Features:** upright, columnar or spreading, evergreen tree; foliage; bark; cones; habit
**Height:** 60 cm–35 m (2–115')
**Spread:** 60 cm–18 m (2–60')
**Hardiness:** zones 2–8

# Potentilla
*Potentilla*

*P. fruticosa* (above & below)

Potentilla is fuss-free and blooms madly all summer. The cheery, yellow-flowered varieties are usually seen, but cultivars with flowers in shades of white, pink, red and tangerine have broadened its use.

## Growing

Potentilla prefers **full sun** but will tolerate partial or light shade. The soil should be of **poor to average fertility** and **well drained**. This plant tolerates most conditions, including sandy or clay soil and wet or dry conditions. Established plants are drought tolerant. Too much fertilizer or too rich a soil will encourage weak, floppy, disease-prone growth.

## Tips

Potentilla is useful in a shrub or mixed border. The smaller cultivars can be included in rock gardens and on rock walls. On slopes that are steep or awkward to mow, potentilla can prevent soil erosion and reduce the time spent maintaining the lawn. It can even be used to form a low, informal hedge.

## Recommended

Of the many cultivars of *P. fruticosa,* the following are a few of the most popular and interesting. '**Abbotswood**' is one of the best white-flowered cultivars; '**Goldfinger**' has large, bright yellow flowers; '**Pink Beauty**' bears pink, semi-double flowers; and '**Tangerine**' has orange flowers.

*Orange, red or pink flowers may fade in hot weather or direct sunlight. Consider planting cultivars that bloom in these colours in partial or light shade. In any case, flower colours should improve in fall, when the weather cools down.*

**Also called:** shrubby cinquefoil  **Features:** mounding, deciduous shrub; flowers; foliage; habit  **Height:** 30 cm–1.5 m (1–5')  **Spread:** 30 cm–1.5 m (1–5')  **Hardiness:** zones 2–8

# Rhododendron • Azalea

*Rhododendron*

*R. 'Purple Gem'*

Even when not covered in a stunning display of brightly coloured flowers, rhododendrons are wonderful landscape plants.

## Growing

Rhododendrons and evergreen azaleas grow best in **partial shade** or **light shade** while the deciduous azaleas typically grow best in **full sun** or **partial shade**. Choose a location that is protected from drying winter winds and avoid hot, sun-scorched locations. The soil should be **fertile, humus rich, acidic, moist** and **well drained**. A good mulch is important to keep the soil moist and to protect the shallow roots of these plants.

## Tips

Rhododendrons and azaleas perform best and look their best when planted in groups. Use them in shrub or mixed borders, in woodland gardens and in sheltered rock gardens. Annual fertilizing with acid-loving plant food helps keep the soil acidic, which is essential for rhododendron and azalea health.

## Recommended

These bushy shrubs vary greatly in size and hardiness, may be evergreen or deciduous and bear flowers in a huge range of colours. Hundreds of rhododendron and azalea species, hybrids and cultivars are available. Visit your local garden centre or specialty grower to see what is available. Two popular and hardy hybrids are **'Hellikki,'** a dense, rounded plant with violet-red flowers, and **'Olga Mezzitt,'** an evergreen plant with peachy pink flowers and red fall foliage.

**Features:** upright, mounding, rounded, evergreen or deciduous shrub; spring flowers; foliage; habit **Height:** 60 cm–3.6 m (2–12') **Spread:** 60 cm–3.6 m (2–12') **Hardiness:** zones 3–8

# Serviceberry
## *Amelanchier*

*A. canadensis* (above)

*Serviceberry fruit can be used in place of blueberries in any recipe, having a similar but generally sweeter flavour.*

The *Amelanchier* species are first-rate North American natives, bearing lacy, white flowers in spring, followed by edible berries. In fall the foliage colour ranges from glowing apricot to deep red.

### Growing
Serviceberries grow well in **full sun** or **light shade**. They prefer soil that is **acidic, fertile, humus rich, moist** and **well drained**. Established plants adapt to periodic droughts.

### Tips
With spring flowers, edible fruit, attractive leaves that turn red in fall and often artistic branch growth, serviceberries make beautiful specimen plants or even shade trees in small gardens. The shrubbier forms can be grown along the edge of a woodland or in a border. In the wild these trees are often found growing near water sources and are beautiful beside ponds or streams.

### Recommended
Several species and hybrids are available. A few popular serviceberries are ***A. arborea*** (downy serviceberry, Juneberry), a small, single- or multi-stemmed tree; ***A. canadensis*** (shadblow serviceberry), a large, upright, suckering shrub; and ***A.* x *grandiflora*** (apple serviceberry), a small, spreading, often multi-stemmed tree. All three have white flowers, purple fruit and good fall colour.

**Also called:** billberry, saskatoon, juneberry
**Features:** single- or multi-stemmed, deciduous large shrub or small tree; spring or early-summer flowers; edible fruit; fall colour; habit; bark **Height:** 1.2–9 m (4–30')
**Spread:** 1.2–9 m (4–30')
**Hardiness:** zones 3–8

# Smoketree

*Cotinus*

*C. coggygria* (above & below)

Bright fall colour, adaptability, flowers of differing colours and variable sizes and forms make smoketree and all its cultivars excellent additions to the garden.

## Growing

Smoketree grows well in **full sun** or **partial shade**. It prefers soil of **average fertility** that is **moist** and **well drained**, but it will adapt to all but very wet soils.

## Tips

Smoketree can be used in a shrub or mixed border, as a single specimen or in groups. It is a good choice for a rocky hillside planting. Branch tips are typically winterkilled in Maritime winters. Branches should be pruned back to the first living bud as they sprout in early June.

## Recommended

*C. coggygria* **'Royal Purple'** is a bushy, rounded shrub with striking, dusky purple foliage that occasionally develops large, puffy plumes of purplish flowers.

**Also called:** smokebush **Features:** bushy, rounded, spreading, deciduous tree or shrub; early-summer flowers; summer and fall foliage **Height:** 3–4.5 m (10–15') **Spread:** 3–4.5 m (10–15') **Hardiness:** zones 4–8

# Spirea
*Spiraea*

*S. x bumalda* cultivar (above), *S. x vanhouttei* (below)

Spireas, seen in so many gardens and with dozens of cultivars, remain undeniable favourites. With a wide range of forms, sizes and colours of both foliage and flowers, spireas have many possible uses in the landscape.

## Growing

Spireas prefer **full sun**. To help prevent foliage burn, provide protection from very hot afternoon sun. The soil should be **fertile, acidic, moist** and **well drained**.

## Tips

Spireas are used in shrub or mixed borders, in rock gardens and as informal screens and hedges. In late fall or early spring, shear the round forms down to a 60 cm (24") ball and thin out older stems to the ground.

## Recommended

Many species and cultivars of spirea are available. The following are two popular hybrid groups. **S. x bumalda** (S. japonica 'Bumalda') is a low, broad, mounded shrub with pink flowers. It is rarely grown in favour of the many cultivars, which also have pink flowers, but often brightly coloured foliage as well. **S. x vanhouttei** (bridal wreath spirea, Vanhoutte spirea) is a dense, bushy shrub with arching branches that bears clusters of white flowers. Check at your local nursery or garden centre to see what cultivars are available.

**Features:** round, bushy, deciduous shrub; summer flowers; habit **Height:** 30 cm–3 m (1–10') **Spread:** 30 cm–3.6 m (1–12') **Hardiness:** zones 3–8

# Spruce

*Picea*

Spruce trees are one of the most commonly grown and commonly abused evergreens. Grow spruces where they have enough room to spread; then let them branch all the way to the ground.

## Growing

Spruce trees grow best in **full sun**. The soil should be **deep, moist, well drained** and **neutral to acidic**. These trees generally don't like hot, dry or polluted conditions, although many are grown in these conditions and appear to adapt quite well. Spruces are best grown from small, young stock, as they dislike being transplanted when larger or more mature.

## Tips

Spruces are used as specimen trees. The dwarf and slow-growing cultivars can also be used in shrub or mixed borders. These trees look most attractive when allowed to keep their lower branches.

## Recommended

Spruces are generally upright, pyramidal trees, but cultivars may be low-growing, wide-spreading or even weeping in habit. *P. abies* (Norway spruce), *P. abies* **'Nidiformis'** (nest spruce), *P. glauca* (white spruce), *P. glauca* **'Albertiana Conica'** (dwarf Alberta spruce), *P. omorika* (Serbian spruce), *P. pungens* (Colorado spruce) and *P. pungens* **'Glauca Globosa'** (globe blue spruce) are popular and commonly available species and cultivars. Many more cultivars are also available.

*P. glauca* 'Albertiana Conica' (above)
*P. pungens* var. *glauca* 'Moerheim' (below)

*Oil-based pesticides such as dormant oil can take the blue out of your blue-needled spruces. Growth that fills in after this will have the blue colour.*

**Features:** conical or columnar, evergreen tree or shrub; foliage; cones; habit **Height:** 60 cm–24 m (2–80') **Spread:** 60 cm–7.5 m (2–25') **Hardiness:** zones 2–8

# Summersweet Clethra
*Clethra*

Summersweet clethra is one of the best shrubs for adding fragrance to your garden and attracting butterflies and other pollinators.

## Growing
Summersweet clethra grows best in **light shade** or **partial shade**. The soil should be **fertile, humus rich, acidic, moist** and **well drained**.

## Tips
Although not aggressive, this shrub tends to sucker, forming a colony of stems. Use it in a border or in a woodland garden. The light shade along the edge of a woodland is also an ideal location.

## Recommended
*C. alnifolia* is a large, rounded, upright, colony-forming shrub. It grows 90 cm–2.4 m (3–8') tall, spreading 90 cm–1.8 m (3–6') and bearing attractive spikes of white flowers in mid- to late summer. The foliage turns yellow in fall. Several cultivars are available, including pink-flowered selections.

*C. alnifolia* 'Paniculata' (above & below)

*Summersweet clethra is useful in damp, shaded gardens, where the late-season flowers are much appreciated.*

**Also called:** sweet pepperbush, sweetspire **Features:** rounded, suckering, deciduous shrub; fragrant, summer flowers; attractive habit; colourful fall foliage **Height:** 60 cm–2.4 m (2–8') **Spread:** 90 cm–2.4 m (3–8') **Hardiness:** zones 3–8

# Viburnum

*Viburnum*

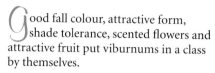

Good fall colour, attractive form, shade tolerance, scented flowers and attractive fruit put viburnums in a class by themselves.

## Growing

Viburnums grow well in **full sun, partial shade** or **light shade**. The soil should be of **average fertility, moist** and **well drained**. Viburnums tolerate both alkaline and acidic soils.

These plants will look neatest if dead-headed, but this practice will of course prevent fruits from forming. Fruiting is better when more than one plant of a species is grown.

## Tips

Viburnums can be used in borders and woodland gardens. They are a good choice for plantings near swimming pools.

## Recommended

Many viburnum species, hybrids and cultivars are available. A few popular ones include **V. dentatum** (arrowwood), an upright, arching, deciduous shrub that bears white flowers in late spring or early summer; **V. lantana** 'Mohican' (Mohican wayfaring tree), a compact, multi-stemmed shrub with white flowers and persistent, showy, red fruit; and **V. trilobum** (American cranberrybush, highbush cranberry), a dense, rounded shrub with clusters of white flowers followed by edible, red fruit.

*V. lantana* 'Mohican' (above & below)

*The edible, but very tart, fruits of* V. trilobum *are popular for making jellies, pies and wine. They can be sweetened somewhat by freezing them before using them or by picking them after the first frost or two.*

---

**Features:** bushy or spreading, evergreen, semi-evergreen or deciduous shrub; flowers (some fragrant); summer and fall foliage; fruit; habit **Height:** 50 cm–6 m (20"–20')
**Spread:** 50 cm–4.5 m (20"–15')
**Hardiness:** zones 3–8

# Weigela
## *Weigela*

*W. florida* 'Polka' (above), *W. florida* cultivar (below)

Weigelas have been improved through breeding, and specimens with more compact forms, longer flowering periods and greater cold tolerance are now available.

### Growing
Weigelas prefer **full sun** but tolerate partial shade. The soil should be **fertile** and **well drained**. These plants will adapt to most well-drained soil conditions.

### Tips
Weigelas can be used in shrub or mixed borders, in open woodland gardens and as informal barrier plantings.

### Recommended
***W. florida*** is a spreading shrub with arching branches that bears clusters of dark pink flowers. Many hybrids and cultivars are available, including dwarf varieties, red-, pink- or white-flowered varieties and varieties with purple, bronze or yellow foliage.

*Weigela is one of the longest-blooming shrubs, with the main flush of blooms lasting as long as six weeks. It often re-blooms if sheared lightly after the first flowers fade. The flowers are very attractive to hummingbirds.*

**Features:** upright or low, spreading, deciduous shrub; late-spring to early-summer flowers; foliage; habit **Height:** 30 cm–2.7 m (1–9') **Spread:** 30 cm–2.7 m (1–9') **Hardiness:** zones 3–8

# Willow

*Salix*

These fast-growing, deciduous shrubs or trees can have colourful or twisted stems or foliage, and they come in a huge range of growth habits and sizes.

## Growing

Willows grow best in **full sun**. The soil should be of **average fertility, moist** and **well drained**, though some of the shrubby species are drought resistant. Avoid planting weeping willow and other willows that are susceptible to willow blight.

## Tips

Large tree willows should be reserved for large spaces and look particularly attractive near water features. Smaller willows can be used as small specimen trees or in shrub and mixed borders. Small and trailing forms can be included in rock gardens and along retaining walls.

## Recommended

The following are just a few of the many popular willows available. **S. arctica** (Arctic willow) is a fast-growing, medium-sized shrub, suitable for hedging. **S. integra** '**Hakuro Nishiki**' (dappled willow, Japanese dappled willow) is a spreading shrub with supple, arching branches that appear to be almost weeping. The young shoots are orange-pink in colour and the leaves are dappled green, cream and pink (zones 5–8). **S. SCARLET CURLS** (S. 'Sarcuzam') is an upright, shrubby tree with curled and twisted branches and leaves. The young stems

*S. integra* 'Hakuro Nishiki' (above)

are reddish and become redder after a frost, creating an attractive winter display of twisted, red shoots (zones 5–8).

---

**Features:** bushy or arching shrub or spreading or weeping tree; summer and fall foliage; stems; habit **Height:** 30 cm–20 m (1–65') **Spread:** 90 cm–20 m (3–65') **Hardiness:** zones 3–8

# Yew

*Taxus*

*T.* x *media* 'Sunburst' (above), *T.* x *media* (below)

From sweeping hedges to commanding specimens, yews can serve many purposes in the garden. They are the most reliable evergreens for deep shade.

## Growing

Yews grow well in any light conditions from **full sun to full shade**. The soil should be **fertile, moist** and **well drained**. These trees tolerate windy, dry and polluted conditions and soils of any acidity. They dislike excessive heat, however, and on the hotter south or southwest side of a building they may suffer needle scorch.

## Tips

Yews can be used in borders or as specimens, hedges, topiary and groundcover. Deer absolutely love yews, so bear that in mind when choosing a location.

Male and female flowers are borne on separate plants. Both must be present for the attractive red arils (seed cups) to form.

## Recommended

***T.* x *media*** (English Japanese yew), a cross between *T. baccata* (English yew) and *T. cuspidata* (Japanese yew), has the vigour of the English yew and the cold hardiness of the Japanese yew. It forms a rounded, upright tree or shrub, though the size and form can vary amongst the many cultivars.

**Features:** evergreen; conical or columnar tree or bushy or spreading shrub; foliage; habit; red seed cups (arils) **Height:** 30 cm–21 m (1–70') **Spread:** 30 cm–9 m (1–30') **Hardiness:** zones 4–8

# Alexander Mackenzie

Explorer Shrub Rose

Alexander Mackenzie is known for its beauty, fragrance and outstanding disease resistance. It bears clusters of fragrant, deep red flowers throughout the summer months and well into fall.

## Growing

Alexander Mackenzie prefers **full sun**. The soil should be **fertile, humus rich, moist** and **well drained**. Deadhead to keep plants tidy and to prolong the blooming period. Trim back any growth that shows winter damage in spring.

## Tips

Alexander Mackenzie makes a lovely specimen plant and can be combined with other roses, shrubs or perennials in a mixed border.

## Recommended

*Rosa* 'Alexander Mackenzie' is a tall, upright shrub bearing clusters of fragrant, double flowers. The thorny stems are tinged reddish purple and the foliage is light green and glossy. This rose is extremely hardy, vigorous and resistant to powdery mildew and black spot.

*Sir Alexander Mackenzie was a noted explorer and fur trader. In 1793 he became the first European to cross the North American continent and reach the Pacific Ocean.*

**Features:** hardy, deciduous shrub; light raspberry-scented, deep red with hot pink blooms in spring and late summer
**Height:** 1.5–2.1 m (5–7')
**Spread:** 1.5–2.1 m (5–7')
**Hardiness:** zones 3–8

# Apothecary's Rose

## Species Rose

*This rose is known for its culinary and medicinal value and for its use in crafts, particularly in potpourri.*

This rose has been cultivated since the 13th century and was used in herbal medicine to treat inflammation, aches, pains and insomnia.

### Growing

Apothecary's Rose prefers **full sun** but tolerates afternoon shade. The soil should be **average to fertile, slightly acidic, humus rich, moist** and **well drained**. The suckers produced should be removed once flowering is complete.

### Tips

Apothecary's Rose can be grown as a specimen, in a shrub border or as a hedge. It can be naturalized or used to prevent soil erosion on a bank too steep for mowing. The flowers are very fragrant, so plant this shrub near windows, doors and frequently used pathways.

### Recommended

*Rosa gallica* 'officinalis' is a bushy, rounded, vigorous, disease-resistant shrub with bristly stems and dark green leaves. One flush of semi-double flowers is produced each year in late spring or early summer. *Rosa gallica* 'Versicolor' has white or light pink flowers with darker pink splashes and stripes.

**Also called:** Red Damask, Red Rose of Lancaster **Features:** rounded habit; fresh and intensely fragrant, crimson purple or pinkish red flowers in early summer; dark red hips **Height:** 75 cm–1.2 m (30"–4') **Spread:** 75 cm–1.2 m (30"–4') **Hardiness:** zones 4–8

# Belle Amour

## Old Garden Rose

Classified as an ancient damask rose, Belle Amour is extremely easy to grow, even in the worst soil or environmental conditions.

### Growing
Belle Amour grows best in **full sun**. The soil should be **average to fertile, humus rich, slightly acidic, moist** and **well drained**, but this rose tolerates most soil conditions once established.

### Tips
Old garden roses like Belle Amour seem most at home in an English country-style garden, but they can be used in borders and as specimens. Plant them where you will be able to enjoy the fragrance of the blooms.

### Recommended
*Rosa* **'Belle Amour'** is an upright shrub with grey-green foliage. It bears fully double, camellia-like blooms in a single flush in late spring or early summer. The bright red hips persist into winter.

*Old garden roses are those that were discovered or hybridized before 1867, and they are admired for their delicate beauty, old-fashioned appearance and fantastic fragrance. They are the ancestors of many roses found today.*

*Some claim that Belle Amour is a cross between an Alba and a Damask Rose.*

**Features:** upright habit; light to medium pink, early-summer flowers with a spicy, myrrh-like scent; red hips **Height:** 1.5–1.8 m (5–6') **Spread:** 90 cm–1.2 m (3–4') **Hardiness:** zones 3–8

# Bonica
Modern Shrub Rose

In 1987 Bonica was named an All-America Selection. It was the first modern shrub rose to receive this honour.

## Growing

Bonica grows best in **full sun** but tolerates some shade. The soil should be **average to fertile, humus rich, slightly acidic, moist** and **well drained**, but this rose adapts to most soils, even soils of low fertility.

## Tips

This versatile rose can be used as a specimen plant, trained to form a standard, grown in containers or used to create a hedge. It will also do well in large mixed containers and in mixed beds and borders.

## Recommended

*Rosa* **'Bonica'** is a rounded to sprawling, repeat-blooming rose with semi-glossy, bright green leaves. It bears semi-double flowers all summer that ripen to bright orange hips in fall. Bonica is disease resistant.

*Bonica is loved by gardeners everywhere for its long blooming period, disease resistance and versatility.*

**Features:** sprawling habit; lightly scented, semi-double, light pink, summer flowers; bright orange, persistent hips  **Height:** 90 cm–1.5 m (3–5') **Spread:** 1–1.2 m (3–4')
**Hardiness:** zones 4–8

# George Vancouver

### Explorer Shrub Rose

George Vancouver is an attractive, compact rose that bears an abundance of blooms repeatedly from early summer through early fall.

## Growing
George Vancouver prefers **full sun**. The soil should be **average to fertile, humus rich, moist** and **well drained**. Deadheading will encourage more prolific repeat blooming.

## Tips
George Vancouver makes an excellent addition to a mixed border and can be used to create a low hedge. It also makes an attractive specimen plant in a small garden.

## Recommended
*Rosa* 'George Vancouver' is a mound-forming shrub that maintains a neat, rounded habit. The double flowers may be borne singly or in clusters of up to six.

*George Vancouver, the explorer for whom this rose is named, made a detailed survey of the West Coast from 1792 to 1794.*

**Features:** compact habit; medium red, double flowers produced in waves from early summer through early fall **Height:** 60–75 cm (24–30") **Spread:** 60–75 cm (24–30") **Hardiness:** zones 3–8

# Hansa

## Rugosa Shrub Rose

Hansa, first introduced in 1905, is one of the most durable, long-lived and versatile roses.

## Growing

Hansa grows best in **full sun**. The soil should preferably be **average to fertile, humus rich, slightly acidic, moist** and **well drained**, but this durable rose adapts to most soils from sandy to silty clay. Remove a few of the oldest canes every few years to keep plants blooming vigorously.

## Tips

Rugosa roses like Hansa make good additions to mixed borders and beds and can also be used as hedges or as specimens. They are often used on steep banks to prevent soil erosion. Their prickly branches deter people from walking across flower beds and compacting the soil.

## Recommended

*Rosa* '**Hansa**' is a bushy shrub with arching canes and leathery, deeply veined, bright green leaves. The double flowers are produced all summer. The bright orange hips persist into winter. Other rugosa roses include '**Blanc Double de Coubert,**' which produces white, double flowers all summer.

**Features:** dense, arching habit; clove-scented, mauve-purple or mauve-red, early-summer to fall flowers; orange-red hips **Height:** 1.2–1.5 m (4–5') **Spread:** 1.5–1.8 m (5–6') **Hardiness:** zones 3–8

# Henry Kelsey
## Explorer Shrub Rose

This vigorous rose can be trained as a climber or grown as an impressive, arching specimen.

### Growing
Henry Kelsey grows best in **full sun**. The soil should be **average to fertile, humus rich, moist** and **well drained**. Although this rose is resistant to powdery mildew and rust, it is sometimes affected by blackspot. Grow it in an area with good air circulation and clear up fallen leaves in fall.

### Tips
Henry Kelsey is frequently grown as a climbing rose; its long, arching canes look very attractive when grown on a trellis against a wall or over an arch or small arbour. At the back of a large border it makes an impressive specimen plant.

### Recommended
*Rosa* **'Henry Kelsey'** is a large, vigorous shrub with long, arching stems and glossy, dark green foliage. It bears large clusters of fragrant, red flowers. It recovers well from cold, snowless winters, sprouting back from low on the plant when the canes are severely killed back.

*This rose was named after a British explorer who expanded the trade routes of the Hudson's Bay Company.*

**Features:** clusters of fragrant, semi-double, bright red or dark pink flowers from summer to fall; dark green, glossy foliage
**Height:** 1.8–2.4 m (6–8')
**Spread:** 1.8 m (6')
**Hardiness:** zones 2–8

# John Cabot
Explorer Shrub Rose

John Cabot was introduced in 1978 as the first climbing Explorer rose and is still considered one of the best in the series.

## Growing
John Cabot grows best in **full sun** but tolerates some afternoon shade. The soil should be **average to fertile, humus rich, slightly acidic, moist** and **well drained**. Deadhead to keep plants tidy. Trim back any tips that show winter damage in spring.

## Tips
John Cabot is best trained as a climber but performs equally well when pruned to form a shrub. Train the branches to climb on a decorative support such as a pergola, archway, fence or obelisk. This rose also looks attractive in mixed beds or borders, especially when it has room to display its open, cascading habit.

## Recommended
*Rosa* 'John Cabot' has bright green foliage and produces profuse, semi-double flowers all summer.

*This rose was named after the first European since the Vikings to explore the mainland of North America and search for the Northwest Passage.*

**Features:** trailing habit; sweet-scented, bright pink or magenta, mid-summer to fall flowers **Height:** 2.4–3 m (8–10') **Spread:** 1.5–1.8 m (5–6') **Hardiness:** zones 3–8

# John Davis

### Explorer Shrub Rose

Introduced in 1986, John Davis has a trailing habit and is one of the longest blooming of the Explorer roses.

### Growing

John Davis grows best in **full sun**. The soil should be **average to fertile, humus rich, moist** and **well drained**, though this rose is tolerant of most growing conditions and even does well in exposed locations.

### Tips

John Davis is an excellent choice for creating a windbreak or hedge. It makes a lovely specimen plant and can be grouped with other plants in a mixed border where its tall, arching canes can be trained against a wall or fence to create a fantastic backdrop. It is often trained as a climber against walls and fences and over small arbours.

### Recommended

*Rosa* '**John Davis**' is a vigorous, trailing rose with dark green, glossy foliage. Blooms are produced in waves from spring to fall. This rose is disease resistant, though leafhoppers and sawflies have been known to damage the foliage. Keep an eye out and catch problems early.

*This rose was named after a 16th-century explorer whose book detailing his final voyage, the* Traverse Book, *became the model for present-day shipping logs.*

**Features:** clusters of lightly scented, double flowers that are pink with a touch of yellow at the petal bases; glossy, dark green foliage; trailing habit
**Height:** 1.8–2.4 m (6–8')
**Spread:** 1.8 m (6')
**Hardiness:** zones 2b–8

# Morden Centennial

Parkland Shrub Rose

This rose was released in 1980 to commemorate the centennial of Morden, Manitoba, and is a tribute to the fantastic research done there to find and develop plants hardy enough to thrive in even the coldest parts of Canada.

### Growing
Morden Centennial grows best in **full sun**. The soil should be **average to fertile, humus rich, moist** and **well drained**. Deadhead the entire flower cluster at once when the blooms are finished to encourage the plant to bloom continuously. As the end of summer nears you may want to stop deadheading and allow some of the hips to develop to provide winter interest.

### Tips
This prolific bloomer produces flowers on new wood, so it will bloom even if it has suffered some dieback over the winter. It makes a lovely addition to a mixed border.

### Recommended
*Rosa* '**Morden Centennial**' is a broad, mound-forming shrub. It produces clusters of bright pink flowers all summer. Plants are susceptible to disease if they become stressed.

*The Parkland roses, developed in Manitoba to withstand cold prairie winters, include a range of cultivars with an excellent selection of flower colours.*

**Features:** clusters of medium to bright pink, double flowers borne on new wood all summer; bright red hips; mound-forming habit
**Height:** 60–90 cm (24–36")
**Spread:** 90 cm–1.2 m (3–4')
**Hardiness:** zones 3–8

# Rosa glauca
## Species Rose

This species rose is a gardener's dream; it's hardy and disease resistant, with striking foliage in summer and colourful hips in winter.

## Growing

*Rosa glauca* grows best and develops contrasting foliage colour in **full sun** but tolerates some shade. The soil should be **average to fertile, humus rich, slightly acidic, moist** and **well drained**, but this rose adapts to most soils, from sandy to silty.

Remove a few of the oldest canes to the ground every few years to encourage younger, more colourful stems to grow in. Removing spent flowers won't prolong the blooming period, and the more flowers you leave, the more hips will form.

## Tips

With its unusual foliage colour, *Rosa glauca* makes a good addition to mixed borders and beds, and it can also be used as a hedge or specimen.

## Recommended

***Rosa glauca*** (*R. rubrifolia*) is a bushy shrub with arching, purple-tinged canes and delicate, purple-tinged, blue-green leaves. The single, star-like flowers bloom in clusters in late spring. The dark red hips persist through winter.

**Also called:** Red-leaved Rose **Features:** dense, arching habit; purple- or red-tinged foliage; late-spring, mauve pink flowers with white centres; persistent, dark red hips **Height:** 1.8–3 m (6–10') **Spread:** 1.5–1.8 m (5–6') **Hardiness:** zones 2–8

# Therese Bugnet

Rugosa Shrub Rose

One of the hardiest roses in the world, Therese Bugnet was developed in Alberta and can withstand winter temperatures down to -37° C (-35° F).

## Growing

Therese Bugnet grows best in full sun but tolerates partial shade. The soil should be average to fertile, humus rich, moist and well drained, though rocky, sandy and clay soils are tolerated. It also tolerates cold, heat, wind and late frosts.

*Therese Bugnet was developed in Alberta by George Bugnet, who invested over 25 years in its development and then named it after his daughter.*

## Tips

Therese Bugnet makes a good addition to mixed borders and beds and can be used as an informal hedge or as a specimen plant. On steep or exposed slopes it can help prevent soil erosion. The fragrance of the flowers can be enjoyed when it is planted alongside paths and walkways.

## Recommended

*Rosa* '**Therese Bugnet**' is a bushy shrub with arching canes that turn cherry red in fall and smooth, grey-green leaves that develop a bronze colouring in fall. The lilac-pink, double flowers are produced all summer, and the hips turn bright orange in fall.

**Also called:** Theresa Bugnet  **Features:** dense, arching habit; clove-scented, early-summer to fall, lilac-pink flowers; bright orange hips
**Height:** 1.5–1.8 m (5–6')
**Spread:** 1.5–1.8 m (5–6')
**Hardiness:** zones 2–8

# William Baffin

Explorer Shrub Rose

ough and versatile, William Baffin is highly disease resistant and requires very little maintenance. It is considered one of the best shrub or climbing roses for cold climates.

## Growing

William Baffin prefers **full sun** but tolerates afternoon shade. The soil should be **average to fertile, humus rich, moist** and **well drained**. This rose does not need winter protection and rarely needs pruning. Trim back any unappealing growth or dead tips in spring.

## Tips

William Baffin can be grown as a large specimen plant or trained to form a pillar or climbing rose. It is hardy enough to survive the winter unprotected when grown on a trellis, arbour or pergola.

## Recommended

*Rosa* 'William Baffin' is a vigorous rose with long, sturdy canes. It has glossy, green foliage and bears large clusters of semi-double flowers in summer and again in fall. It grows much taller in warmer climates than in cold ones.

*This rose was named after the explorer who discovered Lancaster Sound in 1616 on a voyage that took him and Robert Bylot farther north than any other explorer would go for the next 236 years.*

**Features:** vigorous, hardy climber; lightly scented, semi-double, deep pink, summer flowers that repeat in fall
**Height:** 2.4–3 m (8–10')
**Spread:** 1.5–1.8 m (5–6')
**Hardiness:** zones 2–8

# Black-Eyed Susan Vine
*Thunbergia*

Black-eyed Susan vine is a useful, annual flowering vine whose simple flowers dot the plant, giving it a cheerful, welcoming appearance.

## Growing

Black-eyed Susan vines do well in **full sun, partial shade** or **light shade**. Grow them in **fertile, moist, well-drained** soil that is **high in organic matter**.

## Tips

Black-eyed Susan vines can be trained to twine up and around fences, walls, trees and shrubs. They are also attractive trailing down from the top of a rock garden or rock wall or growing in mixed containers and hanging baskets.

## Recommended

*T. alata* is a vigorous, twining climber. It bears yellow flowers, often with dark centres, in summer and fall. Cultivars with large flowers in yellow, orange or white are available.

*T. alata* 'Red Shades' (above), *T. alata* (below)

*Plants grown in containers and hanging baskets can be brought indoors for the winter if acclimated to the lower light levels and kept in a bright, cool location.*

**Features:** twining habit; yellow, orange, violet-blue or creamy white, dark-centred flowers **Height:** 1.5 m (5') or more **Spread:** 1.5 m (5') or more **Hardiness:** tender perennial treated as an annual

# Boston Ivy
## *Parthenocissus*

P. *tricuspidata* 'Lowii' (above)
P. *tricuspidata* 'Fenway Park' (right)

Boston ivy is a handsome vine that establishes quickly and, with patience, provides an air of age and permanence, even on new structures.

### Growing

This vine grows well in any light from **full sun to full shade**. The soil should be **fertile** and **well drained**. Boston ivy will adapt to clay or sandy soils.

### Tips

Boston ivy can cover an entire building, given enough time. It does not require support because it has clinging rootlets that can adhere to just about any surface, even smooth wood, vinyl or metal. Give it lots of space and let it cover a wall, fence or arbour.

### Recommended

*P. tricuspidata* (Boston ivy, Japanese creeper) has dark green, three-lobed leaves that turn red in fall.

*Boston ivy can cover the sides of buildings and help keep them cool in the summer heat. Cut plants back as needed to keep windows and doors accessible.*

**Features:** summer and fall foliage; clinging habit  **Height:** 9–21 m (30–70')
**Spread:** 9–21 m (30–70')
**Hardiness:** zones 4–8

# Clematis
*Clematis*

Clematis is the queen of vines; there are so many species, hybrids and cultivars that it is possible to have one in bloom all season.

### Growing
Clematis plants prefer **full sun** but tolerate partial shade. The soil should be **fertile, humus rich, moist** and **well drained**. These vines enjoy warm, sunny weather, but the roots prefer to be cool. A thick layer of mulch or a planting of low, shade-providing perennials will protect the tender roots. Clematis is quite cold hardy but will fare best when protected from winter wind. The rootball of vining clematis should be planted about 5 cm (2") beneath the surface of the soil.

### Tips
Clematis vines can climb up structures such as trellises, railings, fences and arbours. They can also be allowed to grow over shrubs and up trees and can be used as groundcovers.

### Recommended
There are many species, hybrids and cultivars of clematis. The flower forms, blooming times and sizes of the plants can vary. Check with your local garden centre to see what is available. There are also low-growing shrub and perennial selections of clematis.

C. 'Jackmanii Rubra' (above)
C. 'Gravetye Beauty' (below)

*Try combining a bluish-flowering clematis with a cool pink climbing rose on an arbour—a gorgeous harmony of flower colour.*

**Features:** twining habit; blue, purple, pink, yellow, red or white, early- to late-summer flowers; decorative seedheads
**Height:** 3–5 m (10–16') or more
**Spread:** 1.5 m (5') or more
**Hardiness:** zones 3–8

# Climbing Hydrangea
*Hydrangea*

*H. anomala* subsp. *petiolaris* (above & below)

A mature climbing hydrangea can cover an entire wall, and with its dark, glossy leaves and delicate, lacy flowers, it is quite possibly one of the most stunning climbing plants available.

## Growing

Hydrangea prefers **partial shade** or **light shade** but tolerates both full sun and full shade. The soil should be of **average to high fertility, humus rich, moist** and **well drained**. This plant performs best in cool, moist conditions, so be sure to mulch its roots.

## Tips

Climbing hydrangea climbs up trees, walls, fences, pergolas and arbours. It clings by means of aerial roots, so it needs no narrow supports to twine around, just a somewhat textured surface. It also grows over rocks, can be used as a groundcover and can be trained to form a small tree or shrub.

## Recommended

***H. anomala* subsp. *petiolaris*** (*H. petiolaris*) is a clinging vine with dark, glossy, green leaves that sometimes turn an attractive yellow in fall. For more than a month in mid-summer, the vine is covered with white, lacy-looking flowers, and the entire plant appears to be veiled in a lacy mist.

**Features:** flowers; clinging habit; exfoliating bark **Height:** 15–24 m (50–80') **Spread:** 15–24 m (50–80') **Hardiness:** zones 4–8

# Dutchman's Pipe
## *Aristolochia*

*A. durior* (above & left)

It can be cut back as needed during the growing season and should be thinned to a strong frame of main branches in late fall or spring. The vine dies back in winter, and mulching for added protection is a must.

### Tips
Dutchman's pipe is grown on trellises, arbours and buildings as a quick-growing screen.

### Recommended
**A. macrophylla** (*A. durior,* smooth Dutchman's pipe) is a deciduous, twining vine that bears unusual, pipe-shaped, green flowers with brown, purple and yellow mottling. Some people find the scent of the flowers unpleasant.

For a vigorous climber that provides a thick screen for shade or privacy, look no further than Dutchman's pipe. This plant bears unusual, pipe-shaped flowers that are often hidden behind its dense curtain of large, heart-shaped leaves.

### Growing
Dutchman's pipe grows well in **full sun** or **partial shade**. The soil should be **fertile** and **well drained**. Provide a sturdy support for the vine to twine up.

*Butterflies adore the flowers of Dutchman's pipe.*

**Features:** unusual, exotic flowers; heart-shaped leaves; twining habit; attracts pollinators
**Height:** 6–9 m (20–30')
**Spread:** 1.5–3 m (5–10')
**Hardiness:** zones 5–8

# Hardy Kiwi
## *Actinidia*

Hardy kiwi is handsome in its simplicity. Its lush, green leaves, vigour and adaptability make it very useful, especially on difficult sites.

## Growing

Hardy kiwi vines grow best in **full sun**. The soil should be **fertile** and **well drained**. These plants require shelter from strong winds.

## Tips

Hardy kiwi vines need a sturdy structure to twine around. Pergolas, arbours and sufficiently large and sturdy fences provide good support. Given a trellis against a wall, a tree or some other upright structure, hardy kiwis will twine upward all summer. They can also be grown in containers.

Hardy kiwi vines can grow uncontrollably. Don't be afraid to prune them back if they are getting out of hand.

## Recommended

There are two hardy kiwi vines commonly grown here. **A. arguta** (hardy kiwi, bower actinidia) has dark green, heart-shaped leaves, white flowers and smooth-skinned, greenish yellow, edible fruit. **A. kolomikta** (variegated kiwi vine, kolomikta actinidia) has green leaves strongly variegated with pink and white, white flowers and smooth-skinned, greenish yellow, edible fruit.

A. kolomikta (above), A. arguta (below)

*Both a male and a female vine must be present for fruit to be produced. The plants are often sold in pairs.*

**Features:** early-summer flowers; edible fruit; twining habit **Height:** 4.5–9 m (15–30') to indefinite **Spread:** 4.5–9 m (15–30') to indefinite **Hardiness:** zones 3–8

# Honeysuckle
*Lonicera*

Honeysuckles can be rampant, twining vines, but with careful consideration and placement they won't overrun your garden. The fragrance of the flowers makes any effort worthwhile.

## Growing

Honeysuckles grow well in **full sun** or **partial shade**. The soil should be **average to fertile, humus rich, moist** and **well drained**.

## Tips

Honeysuckles can be trained to grow up a trellis, fence, arbour or other structure. In a large container near a porch it will ramble over the edges of the pot and up the railings with reckless abandon.

## Recommended

There are dozens of honeysuckle species, hybrids and cultivars. Check with your local garden centre to see what is available.

***L. sempervirens*** (trumpet honeysuckle, coral honeysuckle) bears orange or red flowers in late spring and early summer. Many cultivars and hybrids are available with flowers in yellow, red or scarlet, including ***L.* x *brownii* 'Dropmore Scarlet,'** one of the hardiest of the climbing honeysuckles (cold hardy to zone 4). It bears bright orange to orange-red flowers for most of the summer.

*L.* x *brownii* 'Dropmore Scarlet' (above & below)

*Large bumblebees, frustrated at the narrow tube of the flowers, puncture the side of the tube to get at the nectar.*

**Features:** late-spring and early-summer flowers; twining habit; fruit
**Height:** 1.8–6 m (6–20')
**Spread:** 1.8–6 m (6–20')
**Hardiness:** zones 5–8

# Hops
*Humulus*

*I*f you sit nearby for an afternoon, you might actually be able to watch your hops grow.

## Growing

Hops grow best in **full sun**. The soil should be **average to fertile, humus rich, moist** and **well drained**. Established plants will adapt to most conditions as long as they are well watered for the first few years.

## Tips

Hops will quickly twine around any sturdy support to create a screen or to shade a patio or deck. Provide a pergola, arbour, porch rail or even a telephone pole for hops to grow up. Most trellises are too delicate for this vigorous grower.

## Recommended

**H. lupulus** is a fast-growing, twining vine with rough-textured, bright green leaves and stems. The fragrant, cone-like flowers—used to flavour beer—that are produced only on the female plants mature from green to beige. A cultivar with golden yellow foliage is available.

*H. lupulus* (above & below)

*Hops are true perennials; each year the plant sends up shoots from ground level. The previous year's growth will need to be cleared away.*

**Features:** twining habit; dense growth; cone-like, late-summer flowers
**Height:** 3–6 m (10–20') or more
**Spread:** 3–6 m (10–20') or more
**Hardiness:** zones 3–8

# Morning Glory

*Ipomoea*

*I. tricolor* (above & below)

*I. alba, commonly called moonflower, is a twining climber that bears sweet-scented, white flowers that only open at night. It is similar in size and habit to the two morning glories listed to the right.*

Brightly coloured flowers are produced in abundance, giving even the dullest fence or wall a splash of excitement.

### Growing

Morning glory grows best in **full sun**. The soil should be of **poor to average fertility, light** and **well drained**, though the plant adapts to most soil conditions. Morning glory twines around narrow objects to climb and must be provided with a trellis or wires if grown against a fence with broad boards, a wall or any other surface it won't be able to wind around. It resents having its roots disturbed and is best started as seeds planted where you want them to grow.

### Tips

Morning glory can be grown on fences, walls, trees, trellises and arbours. As groundcover, morning glory will grow over any objects it encounters. It can also be grown in hanging baskets or containers where it will spill over the edges. Plants self-seed easily.

### Recommended

*I. purpurea* is a twining climber that bears trumpet-shaped flowers in shades of purple, blue, pink or white. Cultivars are available.

*I. tricolor* is a twining climber that bears trumpet-shaped flowers in shades of blue and purple, often with lighter or white centres. Many cultivars are available, including **'Heavenly Blue,'** with white-centred, sky-blue flowers.

**Features:** fast-growing, twining habit; flowers; foliage **Height:** 2–4 m (7–13')
**Spread:** 2–4 m (7–13')
**Hardiness:** tender annual

# Canna Lily
## *Canna*

Canna lilies are stunning, dramatic plants that give an exotic flair to any garden.

## Growing

Canna lilies grow best in **full sun** in a sheltered location. The soil should be **fertile, moist** and **well drained**. Plant out in spring once the soil has warmed. Plants can be started early indoors in containers to get a head start on the growing season. Deadhead to prolong blooming.

## Tips

Canna lilies can be grown in a bed or border. They make dramatic specimen plants and can even be included in large planters.

## Recommended

A wide range of canna lilies are available, including cultivars and hybrids with green, bronzy, purple or yellow-and-green-striped foliage. Flowers may be white, red, orange, pink, yellow or bicoloured. Dwarf cultivars that grow 45–70 cm (18–28") tall are also available.

*The rhizomes can be lifted after the foliage is killed back in fall. Clean off any clinging dirt, cut off the foliage and store the rhizomes in a cool, frost-free location in slightly moist peat moss. Check on them regularly through the winter—if they start to sprout, pot them and move them to a bright window until they can be moved outdoors.*

C. hybrid (above & below)

---

**Features:** decorative foliage; summer flowers
**Height:** 45 cm–1.8 m (18"–6')
**Spread:** 30–90 cm (12–36") **Hardiness:** zones 7–8; often grown as an annual

# Crocus
*Crocus*

C. x *vernus* cultivars (above & below)

Crocuses are harbingers of spring. They often appear, as if by magic, in full bloom from beneath the melting snow.

## Growing

Crocuses grow well in **full sun** or **light, dappled shade**. The soil should be of **poor to average fertility, gritty** and **well drained**. The corms should be planted about 8 cm (3") deep in fall.

## Tips

Crocuses are almost always planted in groups. Drifts of crocuses can be planted in lawns to provide interest and colour while the grass still lies dormant. In beds and borders they can be left to naturalize. Groups of plants will fill in and spread out to provide a bright welcome in spring.

## Recommended

Many crocus species, hybrids and cultivars are available. The spring-flowering crocus most people are familiar with is *C.* **x** *vernus*, commonly called Dutch crocus. Many cultivars are available with flowers in shades of purple, yellow and white, sometimes bicoloured or with darker veins.

Features: early-spring flowers  Height: 5–15 cm (2–6")  Spread: 5–10 cm (2–4")
Hardiness: zones 3–8

# Daffodil

*Narcissus*

$\mathcal{M}$any gardeners automatically think of large, yellow, trumpet-shaped flowers when they think of daffodils, but there is plenty of variation in colour, form and size among the daffodils.

## Growing

Daffodils grow best in **full sun** or **light, dappled shade**. The soil should be **average to fertile, moist** and **well drained**. Bulbs should be planted in fall, 5–20 cm (2–8") deep depending on the size of the bulb. The bigger the bulb the deeper it should be planted. A rule of thumb is to measure the bulb from top to bottom and multiply that length by three to know how deeply to plant.

## Tips

Daffodils are often planted where they can be left to naturalize in the light shade beneath a tree or in a woodland garden. In mixed beds and borders, the summer foliage of other plants hides the faded leaves. Daffodils are one of the few spring bulbs that deer will absolutely not touch.

## Recommended

Many species, hybrids and cultivars of daffodils are available. Flowers come in shades of white, yellow, peach, orange or pink and may also be bicoloured. Flowers range from 4–15 cm (1 ½–6") across and can be solitary or borne in clusters. There are about 12 flower form categories.

*The cup in the centre of a daffodil is called the corona, and the group of petals that surrounds the corona is called the perianth.*

**Features:** spring flowers **Height:** 10–60 cm (4–24") **Spread:** 10–30 cm (4–12") **Hardiness:** zones 3–8

# Dahlia
*Dahlia*

Mixed cultivars in a cutting bed (above)

*Dahlia cultivars span a vast array of colours, sizes and flower forms, but breeders have yet to develop true blue, scented or frost-hardy selections.*

The variation in size, shape and colour of dahlia flowers is astonishing. You are sure to find at least one that appeals to you.

### Growing

Dahlias prefer **full sun**. The soil should be **fertile, rich in organic matter, moist** and **well drained**. All dahlias are tender, tuberous perennials treated as annuals. Tubers can be purchased and started early indoors. They can also be lifted for storage when the foliage turns black after the first real frost in fall. Store them over winter in a cool, frost-free location, packed loosely in slightly moist peat moss. When the tubers start sprouting in mid- to late winter, pot them and keep them in a bright room. Deadhead to keep plants tidy and blooming.

### Tips

Dahlias make attractive, colourful additions to a mixed border. The smaller varieties make good edging plants and the larger ones make good alternatives to shrubs. Varieties with unusual or interesting flowers are attractive specimen plants.

### Recommended

Of the many dahlia hybrids, most are grown from tubers but a few can be started from seed. Many hybrids are sold based on flower shape, such as collarette, decorative or peony-flowered. The flowers range in size from 5–30 cm (2–12") and are available in shades of purple, pink, white, yellow, orange or red, with some bicoloured. Check with your local garden centre to see what is available.

**Features:** summer flowers; attractive foliage; bushy habit **Height:** 20 cm–1.5 m (8"–5') **Spread:** 20–45 cm (8–18") **Hardiness:** tender perennial grown as an annual

# Flowering Onion

*Allium*

Flowering onions, with their striking, ball-like to loose, nodding clusters of flowers, are sure to attract attention in the garden.

## Growing

Flowering onions grow best in **full sun**. The soil should be **average to fertile, moist** and **well drained**. Plant bulbs in fall, 5–10 cm (2–4") deep depending on the size of the bulb.

## Tips

Flowering onions are best planted in groups in a bed or border where they can be left to naturalize. Most will self-seed when left to their own devices. The foliage, which tends to fade just as the plants come into flower, can be hidden with groundcover or a low, bushy companion plant.

## Recommended

Several flowering onion species, hybrids and cultivars have gained popularity for their decorative pink, purple, white, yellow, blue or maroon flowers. These include **A. aflatunense**, with dense, globe-like clusters of lavender flowers; **A. caeruleum** (blue globe onion), with globe-like clusters of blue flowers; **A. cernuum** (nodding or wild onion), with loose, drooping clusters of pink flowers; and **A. giganteum** (giant onion), a big plant up to 1.8 m (6') tall, with large, globe-shaped clusters of pinky purple flowers.

*A. giganteum* (above), *A. cernuum* (below)

*Although the leaves have an onion scent when bruised, the flowers are often sweetly fragrant. They make a great addition to dried flower arrangements.*

**Features:** striking, often globular, summer flowers; cylindrical or strap-shaped leaves **Height:** 30 cm–1.8 m (1–6') **Spread:** 5–30 cm (2–12") **Hardiness:** zones 3–8

# Gladiolus

*Gladiolus*

Perhaps best known as a cut flower, gladiolus adds an air of extravagance to the garden.

## Growing

Gladiolus grows best in **full sun** but tolerates partial shade. The soil should be **fertile, humus rich, moist** and **well drained**. Flower spikes may need staking and a sheltered location out of the wind to prevent them from blowing over.

Plant corms in spring, 10–15 cm (4–6") deep, once the soil has warmed. Corms can also be started early indoors. Plant a few corms each week for about a month to prolong the blooming period.

## Tips

Planted in groups in beds and borders, gladiolus makes a bold statement. Corms can also be pulled up in fall and stored in damp peat moss in a cool, frost-free location for winter.

## Recommended

**G. x *hortulanus*** is a huge group of hybrids. Gladiolus flowers come in almost every imaginable shade, except blue. Plants are commonly grouped in three classifications: **grandiflorus** is the best known, each corm producing a single spike of large, often ruffled flowers; **nanus**, the hardiest group, can survive in zone 3 with winter protection and produces several spikes of up to seven flowers; and **primulinus**, which produces a single spike of up to 23 flowers that are more spaced out on the spike than those of grandiflorus.

G. x *hortulanus Grandiflorus* (above)
G. 'Homecoming' (below)

*Over 10,000 cultivars of gladiolus have been developed.*

**Features:** brightly coloured, mid- to late-summer flowers **Height:** 50 cm–1.8 m (20"–6') **Spread:** 15–30 cm (6–12") **Hardiness:** zone 8; grown as an annual

# Glory-of-the-Snow

*Chionodoxa*

*A* perfect companion for crocus, glory-of-the-snow brightens the spring garden as the frost retreats.

## Growing

Glory-of-the-snow grows best in **full sun**. The soil should be of **average fertility** and **well drained**. A wet winter soil should be avoided as these plants can quickly develop root or bulb rot. Plant bulbs 8 cm (3") deep in fall.

## Tips

Because these bulbs appreciate dry winter soil, they make a good choice for planting under the overhang of the house. They also make lovely additions to rock and alpine gardens. These plants self-seed and can be left to naturalize.

## Recommended

*C. forbesii* forms a clump of narrow leaves. It bears clusters of 4–12 blue, star-shaped flowers with white centres in early spring. It grows 10–20 cm (4–8") tall and spreads 5–10 cm (2–4").

*C. luciliae* forms a clump of narrow leaves and bears clusters of two or three blue, star-shaped flowers in early spring. It grows up to 15 cm (6") tall and spreads 5–10 cm (2–4").

*C. luciliae* (above), *C. forbesii* (below)

*Confusing glory-of-the-snow with Siberian squill? The former has upward-facing flowers; those of the latter droop downward.*

**Features:** star-shaped, blue, early-spring flowers
**Height:** 10–20 cm (4–8") **Spread:** 5–10 cm (2–4") **Hardiness:** zones 3–8

# Grape Hyacinth
## *Muscari*

*M. botryoides* (above & below)

It's not difficult to see where these bulbs get their common name. The purple or blue flowers, borne densely clustered on spikes, do indeed look like bunches of grapes.

## Growing

Grape hyacinths grow best in **full sun** but tolerate partial shade or light shade. The soil should be **average to fertile, humus rich, moist** and **well drained**. Plant bulbs 7–10 cm (2 ½–4") deep in fall.

## Tips

Planted in masses or small groups, grape hyacinths make great spring accent plants, blending well with other bulbs and spring-blooming plants. They can be left to naturalize in borders and even in lawns, where they create a good excuse for not mowing your lawn in spring.

## Recommended

*M. armeniacum* (Armenian grape hyacinth) forms a low-growing clump of narrow, grass-like leaves. The bright blue or purple flowers are densely clustered on spikes. '**Mt. Hood**' has bicoloured flower clusters. The upper third are white while the lower flowers are blue. '**Valerie Finnis**' bears large spikes of plump, pale blue flowers. Its origin is uncertain and it is sometimes considered a cultivar of *M. neglectum*. (Zones 4–8)

*M. botryoides* (common grape hyacinth) is similar in appearance to Armenian grape hyacinth, but the plants are much smaller. The flowers are pale blue. '**Album**' has white flowers. (Zones 2–8)

*M. comosum* '**Plumosum**' has bright red-violet flowers with feathery rather than grape-like spikes. (Zones 4–8)

**Features:** blue, white, yellow or purple, spring flowers; good for naturalizing **Height:** 10–20 cm (4–8") **Spread:** 15–30 cm (6–12") **Hardiness:** zones 2–8

# Hyacinth
## *Hyacinthus*

*H. orientalis* cultivars (above & below)

These fragrant flowers can be over-powering when grown indoors but are delightful in the garden.

## Growing

Hyacinths grow best in **full sun** but tolerate partial shade. The soil should be of **average fertility, moist** and **well drained**. Plant bulbs 10–20 cm (4–8") deep and 5–8 cm (2–3") apart in fall, four to six weeks before the ground freezes. The colder your winters are the deeper you should plant these bulbs.

## Tips

Plant hyacinths in groups of three to seven amongst the other plants in your beds and borders for a bold splash of colour and an unforgettable fragrance in your spring garden. The fading foliage of the small groups will be hidden as the other plants in the beds fill in for the summer.

## Recommended

**H. orientalis** is a perennial bulb that forms a clump of strap-shaped leaves. A spike of fragrant, star-shaped, light purple flowers is produced in spring. Many cultivars have been developed that come in a huge range of colours, including shades of purple, pink, red, yellow, orange, blue and white.

**Features:** fragrant, spring flowers; long bloom period **Height:** 20–30 cm (8–12")
**Spread:** 7–15 cm (3–6") **Hardiness:** zones 5–9; often treated as an annual

# Lily
## *Lilium*

Decorative clusters of large, richly coloured blooms grace these tall plants. Flowers are produced at differing times of the season, depending on the hybrid, and it is possible to have lilies blooming all season if a variety of cultivars are chosen.

### Growing

Lilies grow best in **full sun** but like to have their roots shaded. The soil should be **rich in organic matter, fertile, moist** and **well drained**.

### Tips

Lilies are often grouped in beds and borders and can be naturalized in woodland gardens and near water features. These plants are narrow and tall; plant at least three plants together to create some volume.

### Recommended

The many species, hybrids and cultivars available are grouped by type. Visit your local garden centre to see what is available. The following are two popular groups of lilies. **Asiatic hybrids** bear clusters of flowers in early summer or mid-summer and are available in a wide range of colours (zones 4–7). **Oriental hybrids** bear clusters of large, fragrant flowers in mid- and late summer. Colours are usually white, pink or red (zones 5–7).

*Lily bulbs should be planted in fall before the first frost, but they can also be planted in spring if bulbs are available.*

L. Asiatic Hybrids (above), L. 'Stargazer' (below)

**Features:** early-, mid- or late-season flowers in shades of orange, yellow, peach, pink, purple, red or white **Height:** 60 cm–1.5 m (2–5') **Spread:** 30 cm (12") **Hardiness:** zones 4–7

# Scilla

*Scilla*

This easy-to-grow spring bloomer looks wonderful in mass plantings and is resistant to browsing by deer.

## Growing

Scilla grows well in **full sun, partial shade** and **light shade**. The soil should be **average to fertile, humus rich** and **well drained**. Bulbs should be planted 7–10 cm (2 ½–4") deep in fall. These plants form clumps that can be dug, divided and moved, like any perennial clump, throughout the season.

## Tips

Scilla makes a lovely addition to mixed beds and borders where the bulbs can be interplanted among the other plants. It can also be planted into lawns, meadow gardens and woodland gardens where it can be left to naturalize.

## Recommended

*S. bifolia* is a low-growing plant with narrow, strap-shaped leaves. It bears clusters of blue or purple flowers in spring. It grows 10–15 cm (4–6") tall and spreads about 8 cm (3"). (Zones 3–8)

*S. scilloides* (Chinese scilla) also has narrow, strap-shaped leaves. It bears large clusters of small, purple-pink flowers in late summer and fall. It grows 15–20 cm (6–8") tall and spreads about 10 cm (4"). (Zones 4–8)

*S. siberica* (Siberian squill, spring squill) has wider strap-shaped leaves than the other two plants. It bears small clusters of bright blue, nodding flowers in spring. It grows 10–20 cm (4–8") tall and spreads about 5 cm (2"). Cultivars are available. (Zones 5–8)

*S. siberica* (above & below)

Also called: squill Features: spring or fall flowers Height: 10–20 cm (4–8") Spread: 5–10 cm (2–4") Hardiness: zones 3–8

# Snowdrops
## *Galanthus*

*G. elwesii* (above), *G. nivalis* (below)

Snowdrops are the first bulbs to bloom with the early melting snow. Their delicate, white, nodding flowers give a glimpse of the still-distant spring.

### Growing

Snowdrops prefer to grow in **partial** or **light shade** but happily tolerate all light conditions from full sun to full shade. The soil should be of **average fertility, humus rich, moist** and **well drained**.

Snowdrops prefer not to have their soil dry out completely in summer. Plant bulbs 10 cm (4") deep and 5 cm (2") apart. Divide or move plants as soon as possible after flowering is complete in spring.

### Tips

Snowdrops are popular bulbs for naturalizing. They can be planted in mixed beds and borders, where they thrive at the foot of deciduous shrubs, and in meadow plantings.

### Recommended

*G. elwesii* (giant snowdrop) forms a clump of bright green, strap-shaped leaves. It bears fragrant, white flowers in late winter and grows 12–30 cm (5–12") tall.

*G. nivalis* (common snowdrop) forms a clump of long, narrow leaves. It bears small, fragrant flowers in winter and grows about 10 cm (4") tall. **'Flore Pleno'** bears double flowers.

**Features:** white, early-spring flowers
**Height:** 10–30 cm (4–12") **Spread:** 5–15 cm (2–6") **Hardiness:** zones 3–8

# Tulip
*Tulipa*

*T.* hybrids (above & below)

Tulips, with their beautiful, often garishly coloured flowers are a welcome sight as we enjoy the warm days of spring.

## Growing

Tulips grow best in **full sun**. The flowers tend to bend toward the light in light shade or partial shade. The soil should be **fertile** and **well drained**. Plant bulbs in fall, 10–15 cm (4–6") deep depending on the size of the bulb. Bulbs that have been cold treated can be planted in spring. Though tulips can repeat bloom, many hybrids perform best if planted new each year. Species and older cultivars are the best choice for naturalizing.

## Tips

Tulips provide the best display when mass planted or planted in groups in flowerbeds and borders. They can also be grown in containers and can be forced to bloom early in pots indoors. Some of the species and older cultivars can be naturalized in meadow and wildflower gardens.

Deer love tulips, often eating them just before blooming begins. Plantskydd®, the blood-based deer repellent, applied weekly during spring, may avert that heartbreak.

## Recommended

There are about 100 species of tulips and thousands of hybrids and cultivars. They are generally divided into 15 groups based on bloom time and flower appearance. Tulips come in dozens of shades, with many bicoloured or multi-coloured varieties. Blue is the only colour not available. Check with your local garden centre in early fall for the best selection.

**Features:** spring flowers **Height:** 15–75 cm (6–30") **Spread:** 5–20 cm (2–8") **Hardiness:** zones 3–8; sometimes treated as annuals

# Basil

*Ocimum*

The sweet, fragrant leaves of fresh basil add a delicious, licorice-like flavour to salads and tomato-based dishes.

## Growing

Basil grows best in a warm, sheltered location in **full sun**. The soil should be **fertile, moist** and **well drained**. Pinch tips regularly to encourage bushy growth. Plant out or direct sow seed after the danger of frost has passed in spring.

## Tips

Although basil will grow best in a warm spot outdoors in the garden, it can be grown successfully in a pot by a bright window indoors to provide you with fresh leaves all year.

## Recommended

*O. basilicum* is one of the most popular culinary herbs. There are dozens of varieties, including ones with large or tiny, green or purple, smooth or ruffled leaves.

*O. basilicum* 'Genovese' and 'Cinnamon' (above)
*O. basilicum* 'Genovese' (below)

*Basil is a good companion plant for tomatoes—both like warm, moist growing conditions, and when you pick tomatoes for a salad you'll also remember to include a few sprigs of basil.*

**Features:** fragrant, decorative leaves
**Height:** 30–60 cm (12–24")
**Spread:** 30–45 cm (12–18")
**Hardiness:** tender annual

# Borage
*Borago*

*B*orage leaves and flowers are both edible, making an interesting addition to salads. The flowers can also be frozen in ice cubes or used to decorate cakes and other desserts.

## Growing

Borage grows well in **full sun** and **partial shade**. Soil should be of **average fertility, light** and **well drained**, though the plant adapts to most conditions. Seed can be sown directly in the garden in spring. Plants resent being transplanted, as they have long taproots, but they recover fairly quickly if moved when young.

Borage is a vigorous self-seeder. Once you have established it in your garden you will never have to plant it again. Young seedlings can be pulled up if they are growing where you don't want them.

## Tips

Borage makes an attractive addition to herb and vegetable gardens as well as to flower beds and borders. The plants should be pinched back when they are young to encourage bushy growth, otherwise they tend to flop over and develop a sprawling habit. Borage attracts bees, butterflies and other pollinators and beneficial insects to the garden.

## Recommended

*B. officinalis* is a bushy plant with bristly leaves and stems. It bears clusters of star-shaped, blue or purple flowers from mid-summer to fall. A white-flowered variety is available.

*B. officinalis* (above & below)

*Leaves are best eaten young, when they are fuzzy rather than bristly.*

**Features:** blue or purple, summer flowers; bristly and edible stems and leaves **Height:** 45–70 cm (18–28") **Spread:** 45–60 cm (18–24") **Hardiness:** self-seeding annual

# Chives
*Allium*

A. schoenoprasum (above & below)

The delicate onion flavour of chives is best enjoyed fresh. Mix chives into dips or sprinkle them on salads and baked potatoes.

### Growing
Chives grow best in **full sun**. The soil should be **fertile, moist** and **well drained**, but chives adapt to most soil conditions. These plants are easy to start from seed, but they do like the soil temperature to stay above 18° C (65° F) before they will germinate, so seeds started directly in the garden are unlikely to sprout before early summer.

### Tips
Chives are decorative enough to be included in a mixed or herbaceous border and can be left to naturalize. In an herb garden, chives should be given plenty of space to allow self-seeding.

### Recommended
*A. schoenoprasum* forms a clump of bright green, cylindrical leaves. Clusters of pinky purple flowers are produced in early and mid-summer. Varieties with white or pink flowers are available.

**Features:** foliage; form; flowers
**Height:** 20–60 cm (8–24") **Spread:** 30 cm
(12") or more **Hardiness:** zones 3–8

# Coriander • Cilantro

*Coriandrum*

Coriander is a multi-purpose herb. The leaves, called cilantro, are used in salads, salsas and soups, and the seeds, called coriander, are used in pies, chutneys and marmalades. Each has a distinct flavour.

## Growing

Coriander prefers **full sun** but tolerates partial shade. The soil should be **fertile, light** and **well drained**. These plants dislike humid conditions and do best during a dry summer.

## Tips

Coriander has pungent leaves and is best planted where people will not have to brush past it. It is, however, a delight to behold when in flower. Add a plant or two here and there throughout your borders and vegetable garden, both for the visual appeal and to attract beneficial insects.

## Recommended

*C. sativum* forms a clump of lacy basal foliage above which large, loose clusters of tiny, white flowers are produced. The seeds ripen in late summer and fall.

*C. sativum* (above & below)

*The delicate, cloud-like clusters of flowers attract pollinating insects such as butterflies and bees as well as abundant predatory insects that will help keep pest insects at a minimum in your garden.*

**Features:** form; foliage; flowers; seeds
**Height:** 45–60 cm (18–24")
**Spread:** 20–45 cm (8–18")
**Hardiness:** tender annual

# Dill
## Anethum

A. graveolens (above & below)

*A popular Scandinavian dish called gravalax is made by marinating a fillet of salmon in brine flavoured with the leaves and seeds of dill.*

Dill leaves and seeds are probably best known for their use as pickling herbs, though they have a wide variety of other culinary uses.

## Growing
Dill grows best in **full sun** in a sheltered location out of strong winds. The soil should be of **poor to average fertility, moist** and **well drained**. Sow seeds every couple of weeks in spring and early summer to ensure a regular supply of leaves. Plants should not be grown near fennel because they will cross-pollinate and the seeds of both plants will lose their distinct flavours.

## Tips
With its feathery leaves, dill is an attractive addition to a mixed bed or border. It can be included in a vegetable garden but does well in any sunny location. It also attracts predatory insects to the garden.

## Recommended
*A. graveolens* forms a clump of feathery foliage. Clusters of yellow flowers are borne at the tops of sturdy stems.

*Dill turns up frequently in historical records as both a culinary and medicinal herb. It was used by the Egyptians and Romans and is mentioned in the Bible.*

**Features:** feathery, edible foliage; yellow, summer flowers; edible seeds **Height:** 60 cm–1.5 m (2–5') **Spread:** 30 cm (12") or more **Hardiness:** annual

# Fennel
## *Foeniculum*

*A*ll parts of fennel are edible and have a distinctive, licorice-like fragrance and flavour. The seeds are commonly used to make a tea that is good for settling the stomach after a large meal.

## Growing

Fennel grows best in **full sun**. The soil should be **average to fertile, moist** and **well drained**. Avoid planting near dill, as cross-pollination reduces seed production and the seed flavour of each becomes less distinct. Fennel will easily self-sow in the garden.

## Tips

Fennel is an attractive addition to a mixed bed or border. It can be included in a vegetable garden but does well in any sunny location. It also attracts pollinators and predatory insects to the garden. To collect seeds, remove the seed-bearing stems before the seeds start to fall off.

## Recommended

*F. vulgare* is a short-lived perennial that is usually treated like an annual. It forms clumps of loose, feathery foliage. Clusters of small, yellow flowers are borne in late summer; seeds ripen in fall. A large, edible bulb forms at the stem base of the biennial **var. *azoricum***. The bulb is popular raw in salads, cooked in soups and stews and roasted like other root vegetables. **'Purpureum'** is similar in appearance to the species but has bronzy purple foliage.

*F. vulgare* (above), *F. vulgare* 'Bronze' (below)

*Fennel has been used for its medicinal and culinary properties since before ancient Greek times.*

---

**Features:** attractive, fragrant foliage; yellow flowers; edible seeds and bulbous stem base **Height:** 60 cm–1.8 m (2–6') **Spread:** 30–60 cm (12–24") **Hardiness:** zones 4–8

# Lavender

*Lavandula*

*L. angustifolia* (above & below)

Lavender is considered the queen of herbs. With both aromatic and ornamental qualities, it makes a valuable addition to any garden.

### Growing

Lavenders grow best in **full sun**. The soil should be **average to fertile, alkaline** and must be **well drained**. Once established, these plants are heat and drought tolerant. Protect plants from winter cold and wind by locating them in a sheltered spot or by mulching them in fall. Plants can be sheared in spring or after flowering.

### Tips

Lavenders are wonderful, aromatic edging plants. They can be planted in drifts, as specimens in small spaces or used to form low hedges.

### Recommended

*L. angustifolia* (English lavender) is a bushy, aromatic plant. It grows about 60 cm (24") tall, with an equal spread. It bears spikes of light purple flowers from mid-summer to fall. The many cultivars include plants with white or pink flowers, silvery grey to olive green foliage and dwarf or compact habits.

**Features:** purple, pink, blue or white, mid-summer to fall flowers; fragrance; evergreen foliage; bushy, rounded habit
**Height:** 20–90 cm (8–36") **Spread:** up to 1.2 m (4') **Hardiness:** zones 5–8

# Mint
*Mentha*

The cool, refreshing flavour of mint lends itself to tea and other hot or cold beverages. Mint sauce, made from freshly chopped leaves, is often served with lamb.

## Growing

Mint grows well in **full sun** and **partial shade**. The soil should be **average to fertile, humus rich** and **moist**. These plants spread vigorously by rhizomes and may need a barrier in the soil to restrict their spread.

## Tips

Mint is a good groundcover for damp spots. It grows well along ditches that may only be periodically wet. It also can be used in beds and borders but may overwhelm less vigorous plants.

The flowers attract bees, butterflies and other pollinators to the garden.

## Recommended

There are many species, hybrids and cultivars of mint. **M. spicata** (spearmint), **M. x piperita** (peppermint) and **M. x piperita citrata** (orange mint) are three of the most commonly grown culinary varieties. There are also more decorative varieties with variegated or curly leaves as well as varieties with unusual, fruit-scented leaves.

M. x *piperita* 'Chocolate' (above)
M. *gracilis* 'Variegata' (decorative variety) (below)

*A few sprigs of fresh mint added to a pitcher of iced tea give it a refreshing zip.*

**Features:** fragrant foliage; purple, pink or white, summer flowers
**Height:** 15–90 cm (6–36")
**Spread:** 60 cm (24") or more
**Hardiness:** zones 4–8

# Oregano • Marjoram
*Origanum*

Oregano and marjoram are two of the best known and most frequently used herbs. They are popular in stuffings, soups and stews, and no pizza is complete until it has been sprinkled with fresh or dried oregano leaves.

## Growing
Oregano and marjoram grow best in **full sun**. The soil should be of **poor to average fertility, neutral to alkaline** and **well drained**. The flowers attract pollinators to the garden.

## Tips
These bushy perennials make a lovely addition to any border and can be trimmed to form low hedges.

## Recommended
*O. majorana* (marjoram) is upright and shrubby with light green, hairy leaves. It bears white or pink flowers in summer and can be grown as an annual where it is not hardy.

*O. vulgare* var. *hirtum* (oregano, Greek oregano) is the most flavourful culinary variety of oregano. The low, bushy plant has hairy, grey-green leaves and bears white flowers. Many other interesting varieties of *O. vulgare* are available, including those with golden, variegated or curly leaves.

*O. vulgare* 'Aureum' (above & below)

*In Greek,* oros *means "mountain" and* ganos *means "joy" or "beauty," so oregano translates as "joy" or "beauty of the mountain."*

**Features:** fragrant foliage; white or pink, summer flowers; bushy habit
**Height:** 30–80 cm (12–32")
**Spread:** 20–45 cm (8–18")
**Hardiness:** zones 5–8

# Parsley
## *Petroselinum*

*P. crispum* (above), *P. crispum* var. *crispum* (below)

Although usually used as a garnish, parsley is rich in vitamins and minerals and is reputed to freshen the breath after garlic- or onion-rich foods are eaten.

## Growing

Parsley grows well in **full sun** or **partial shade**. The soil should be of **average to rich fertility, humus rich, moist** and **well drained**. Direct sow seeds because the plants resent transplanting. If you start seeds early, use peat pots so the plants can be potted or planted out without disruption.

## Tips

Containers of parsley can be kept close to the house for easy picking. The bright green leaves and compact growth habit make parsley a good edging plant for beds and borders.

## Recommended

*P. crispum* forms a clump of bright green, divided leaves. This plant is biennial but is usually grown as an annual because it is the leaves that are desired, not the flowers or seeds. Cultivars may have flat or curly leaves. Flat leaves are more flavourful and curly are more decorative. Dwarf cultivars are also available.

**Features:** attractive foliage  **Height:** 20–60 cm (8–24")  **Spread:** 30–60 cm (12–24")
**Hardiness:** zones 5–8; grown as an annual

# Sage
*Salvia*

Sage is perhaps best known as a flavouring for stuffing, but it has a great range of uses, including in soups, stews, sausages and dumplings.

### Growing
Sage prefers **full sun** but tolerates light shade. The soil should be of **average fertility** and **well drained**. This plant benefits from a light mulch of compost each year. It is drought tolerant once established.

### Tips
Sage is an attractive plant for the border, adding volume to the middle or as an attractive edging or feature plant near the front. Sage can also be grown in mixed planters.

### Recommended
*S. officinalis* is a woody, mounding plant with soft, grey-green leaves. Spikes of light purple flowers appear in early and mid-summer. Many cultivars with attractive foliage are available, including the silver-leaved **'Berggarten,'** the purple-leaved **'Purpurea,'** the yellow-margined **'Icterina'** and the purple, green and cream variegated **'Tricolor.'**

*S. officinalis* 'Icterina' (above)
*S. officinalis* 'Purpurea' (below)

*Sage has been used since at least ancient Greek times as a medicinal and culinary herb and continues to be widely used for both those purposes today.*

**Features:** fragrant, decorative foliage; blue or purple, summer flowers **Height:** 30–60 cm (12–24") **Spread:** 45–90 cm (18–36") **Hardiness:** zones 5–8

# Thyme
### *Thymus*

Thyme is a popular culinary herb used in soups, stews and casseroles and with roasts.

## Growing
Thyme prefers **full sun**. The soil should be **neutral to alkaline** and of **poor to average fertility**. **Good drainage** is essential. It is beneficial to work leaf mould and sharp limestone gravel into the soil to improve structure and drainage.

## Tips
Thyme is useful for sunny, dry locations at the front of borders, between or beside paving stones, on rock gardens and rock walls and in containers.

Once the plants have finished flowering, shear them back by about half to encourage new growth and to prevent the plants from becoming too woody.

## Recommended
*T.* x *citriodorus* (lemon-scented thyme) forms a mound of lemon-scented, dark green foliage. The flowers are pale pink. Cultivars with silver- or gold-margined leaves are available.

*T. vulgaris* (common thyme) forms a bushy mound of dark green leaves. The flowers may be purple, pink or white. Cultivars with variegated leaves are available.

*These plants are bee magnets when blooming; thyme honey is pleasantly herbal and goes very well with biscuits.*

*T. vulgaris* (above), *T.* x *citriodorus* (below)

---

**Features:** bushy habit; fragrant, decorative foliage; purple, pink or white flowers
**Height:** 20–40 cm (8–16") **Spread:** 20–40 cm (8–16") **Hardiness:** zones 4–8

# Christmas Fern

*Polystichum*

*P. acrostichoides* (above & below)

This delightful native fern is at home in a woodland garden and can even be invited indoors and grown as a houseplant.

### Growing

Christmas fern grows well in **partial to full shade**. The soil should be **fertile, humus rich, moist** and **well drained**, though established plants are fairly tolerant of dry conditions. In spring, trim off any fronds that are looking worn out before the new ones emerge.

Divide in spring to propagate your plant, or carefully remove offsets from the base of the plant.

### Tips

This non-invasive fern makes a lovely addition to a moist woodland garden or to the shaded border of a water feature or rock garden. It can be mass planted and left to naturalize in little-used shaded areas of the garden.

### Recommended

*P. acrostichoides* forms a circular clump of arching, evergreen fronds. This plant is native to eastern North America.

*The use of its fronds to decorate during the holidays gave Christmas fern its common name.*

**Features:** evergreen fronds; adaptable
**Height:** 30–45 cm (12–18")
**Spread:** 30–90 cm (12–36")
**Hardiness:** zones 3–8

# Fescue

*Festuca*

This fine-leaved ornamental grass forms tufted clumps that resemble pincushions. Its metallic blue colouring adds an all-season cooling accent to the garden.

## Growing

Fescue thrives in **full sun to light shade**. The soil should be of **average fertility, moist** and **well drained**. Plants are drought tolerant once established. Fescue emerges early in spring, so shear it back to 2.5 cm (1") above the crown in late winter, before new growth emerges. Shear off flower stalks just above the foliage to keep the plant tidy and to prevent self seeding.

## Tips

With its fine-texture and distinct blue colour, this grass can be used as a single specimen in a rock garden or a container planting. Plant fescue in drifts to create a sea of blue or a handsome edge to a bed, border or pathway. It looks attractive in both formal and informal gardens.

*If you enjoy blue grass, you might also like the large, coarse-textured blue oat grass, Helicotrichon sempervirens 'Saphirsprudel' (Sapphire Fountain), which can reach 1.2 m (4') in height when in flower.*

F. glauca 'Elijah Blue' (above), F. glauca (below)

## Recommended

***F. glauca*** forms tidy, tufted clumps of fine, blue-toned foliage and panicles of flowers in May and June. Cultivars and hybrids come in varying heights and in shades ranging from blue to olive green. **'Elijah Blue'** and **'Boulder Blue'** are popular selections.

**Also called:** blue fescue **Features:** blue to blue-green foliage; colour that persists into winter; tufted habit **Height:** 15–30 cm (6–12") **Spread:** 25–30 cm (10–12") **Hardiness:** zones 3–8

# Flowering Fern

*Osmunda*

*O. regalis* (above) *O. cinnamomea* (below)

Ferns have a prehistoric mystique and add a graceful elegance and textural accent to the garden.

## Growing

Flowering ferns prefer **light shade** but tolerate full sun if the soil is consistently moist. The soil should be **fertile, humus rich, acidic** and **moist**. Flowering ferns tolerate wet soil and will spread as offsets form at the plant base.

*Flowering fern's "flowers" are actually its spore-producing sporangia.*

## Tips

These large ferns form an attractive mass when planted in large colonies. They can be included in beds and borders and make a welcome addition to a woodland garden.

## Recommended

*O. cinnamomea* (cinnamon fern) has light green fronds that fan out in a circular fashion from a central point. Bright green, leafless, fertile fronds that mature to cinnamon brown are produced in spring and stand straight up in the centre of the plant.

*O. regalis* (royal fern) forms a dense clump of foliage. Feathery, flower-like, rusty brown, fertile fronds stand out among the sterile fronds. **'Purpurescens'** fronds are purple-red when they emerge in spring and mature to green. This contrasts well with the purple stems.

**Features:** perennial, deciduous fern; decorative fertile fronds **Height:** 75 cm–1.5 m (30"–5') **Spread:** 60–90 cm (24–36") **Hardiness:** zones 2–8

# Fountain Grass

*Pennisetum*

P. setaceum 'Rubrum'

Fountain grass' low maintenance and graceful form make it easy to place. It will soften any landscape, even in winter.

## Growing

Fountain grass thrives in **full sun**. The soil should be of **average fertility** and **well drained**. Plants are drought tolerant once established. Plants may self-seed but are not troublesome. Shear perennial selections back in early spring, and divide them when they start to die out in the centre.

## Tips

Fountain grass can be used as an individual specimen plant, in group plantings and drifts or combined with flowering annuals, perennials, shrubs and other ornamental grasses. Annual selections are often planted in containers or beds for height and stature.

## Recommended

Both perennial and annual fountain grasses exist. Popular perennials include *P. alopecuroides* **'Hameln'** (dwarf perennial fountain grass), a compact cultivar with silvery white plumes and narrow, dark green foliage that turns gold in fall. Annual fountain grasses include *P. setaceum* (annual fountain grass), which has narrow, green foliage and pinkish purple flowers that mature to grey; its cultivar **'Rubrum'** (red annual fountain grass), with broader, deep burgundy foliage and pinkish purple flowers; and *P. glaucum* **'Purple Majesty'** (purple ornamental millet), which has blackish purple foliage and coarse, bottlebrush flowers. Its form resembles a corn stalk.

**Features:** arching, fountain-like habit; silvery pink, dusty rose to purplish black foliage; flowers; winter interest **Height:** 60 cm–1.5 m (2–5') **Spread:** 60–90 cm (2–3') **Hardiness:** zones 5–8 (some species are annuals)

# Japanese Painted Fern
*Athyrium*

*A. niponicum* var. *pictum* (above)
*A. niponicum* 'Burgandy Lace' (below)

Japanese painted ferns are some of the most well-behaved ferns, adding colour and texture to shady spots without growing rampantly out of control.

## Growing

Japanese painted ferns grow well in **full shade, partial shade** or **light shade**. The soil should be of **average fertility, humus rich, acidic** and **moist**. Division is rarely required but can be done to propagate more plants.

## Tips

Japanese painted ferns form an attractive mass of foliage without spreading aggressively the way some ferns tend to. Include them in shade gardens and moist woodland gardens.

## Recommended

*A. niponicum* var. *pictum* forms a clump of dark green fronds with a silvery or reddish metallic sheen. Cultivars with lovely variations in foliage colouring are available.

*With their metallic shades of silver, burgundy and bronze, the colourful foliage of Japanese painted ferns will brighten up any shaded area.*

**Also called:** painted fern  **Features:** clumping habit; lacy, colourful foliage  **Height:** 30–60 cm (12–24")  **Spread:** 30–45 cm (12–18")  **Hardiness:** zones 3–8

# Maidenhair Fern

*Adiantum*

*A. pedatum* (above & below)

These charming and delicate-looking native ferns add a graceful touch to any woodland planting. Their unique habit and texture make them stand out in the garden.

## Growing

Maidenhair ferns grow well in **light shade** or **partial shade** and tolerate full shade. The soil should be of **average fertility, humus rich, slightly acidic** and **moist**. These plants rarely need dividing, but they can be divided in spring to propagate more plants.

## Tips

These lovely ferns will do well in any shaded spot in the garden. Include them in rock gardens, woodland gardens and shaded borders and beneath shade trees.

They also make an attractive addition to a shaded planting next to a water feature or on a slope where the foliage can be seen as it sways in the breeze.

## Recommended

*A. pedatum* forms a spreading mound of delicate, arching fronds. Light green leaflets stand out against the black stems, and the whole plant turns bright yellow in fall. Spores are produced on the undersides of the leaflets.

**Also called:** northern maidenhair
**Features:** deciduous, perennial fern; summer and fall foliage **Height:** 30–60 cm (12–24") **Spread:** 30–60 cm (12–24")
**Hardiness:** zones 2–8

# Miscanthus

*Miscanthus*

M. sinensis var. *purpurescens* (above)
M. sinensis 'Zebrinus' (below)

Miscanthus is one of the most popular and majestic of all the ornamental grasses. Its graceful foliage dances in the wind and makes an impressive sight all year long.

### Growing

Miscanthus prefers **full sun**. The soil should be of **average fertility, moist** and **well drained**. Some selections also tolerate wet soil. All selections are drought tolerant once established.

Leave the foliage in place to provide interest in winter; then cut it back in spring before the new growth starts.

### Tips

Give this magnificent beauty room to spread so you can fully appreciate its form. The plant's height will determine the best place for each selection in the border. It creates a dramatic impact in groups or as a seasonal screen.

### Recommended

There are many available cultivars of **M. sinensis**, all distinguished by the white midrib on the leaf blade. Some popular selections include **'Gracillimus'** (maiden grass), with long, fine-textured leaves; **'Grosse Fontaine'** (large fountain), a tall, wide-spreading, early-flowering selection; **'Morning Light'** (variegated maiden grass), a short and delicate plant with fine, white leaf edges; **var. *purpurescens*** (flame grass), with foliage that turns bright orange in early fall; **'Strictus'** (porcupine grass), a tall, stiff, upright selection with unusual horizontal, yellow bands; and **'Zebrinus'** (zebra grass), an arching grass with horizontal, yellow bands on the leaves.

*The flower heads make an interesting addition to fresh and dried flower arrangements.*

**Also called:** eulalia, Japanese silver grass **Features:** upright, arching habit; colourful summer and fall foliage; late-summer and fall, pink, copper or silver flowers; winter interest **Height:** 1.2–2.4 m (4–8') **Spread:** 60 cm–1.2 m (2–4') **Hardiness:** zones 5–8; zone 4 with protection

# Moor Grass
## *Molina*

M. caerulea subsp. *arundinacea* (above)

Native to damp moors in Europe and parts of Asia, these plants form neat tufts and might just bring a touch of *Wuthering Heights* to your own garden.

### Growing
Moor grass grows well in **full sun and partial shade**. The soil should be of **average fertility, acidic to neutral, moist** and **well drained**. Wet soils are periodically tolerated. Plants can be divided in spring.

### Tips
Moor grass makes an excellent addition to mixed and herbaceous borders. This non-aggressive grass will not spread uncontrollably. It is particularly useful in somewhat shaded gardens where other ornamental grasses fail to thrive.

### Recommended
*M. caerulea* (purple moor grass) forms a dense, mounded clump of narrow leaves with purple bases. It grows 30 cm–1.2 m (1–4') tall and spreads 15–45 cm (6–18"). Long, narrow, flowering stems are produced all summer. The leaves and flowering stems turn bright yellow in fall. **Subsp.** *arundinacea* (tall moor grass) has larger leaves and flowers than the species. It grows 90 cm–1.8 m (3–6') tall and spreads up to 60 cm (24"). Many popular cultivars have been developed from this subspecies, including **'Karl Foerster'** and **'Skyracer.'**

---

**Features:** non-aggressive, clump-forming habit; attractive leaves and flowers **Height:** 30 cm–1.8 m (1–6') **Spread:** 15–60 cm (6–24") **Hardiness:** zones 4–8

# Ostrich Fern

*Matteuccia*

M. struthiopteris (above & below)

*Ostrich fern is grown commercially for its edible fiddleheads. The tightly coiled, new spring fronds taste delicious when boiled until tender and served with butter. Remove the bitter, reddish brown, papery coating before cooking.*

This popular classic fern is revered for its delicious, emerging spring fronds (fiddleheads) and its stately, vase-shaped habit.

## Growing

Ostrich fern prefers **partial shade** or **light shade** but tolerates full shade and even full sun if the soil is kept moist. The soil should be **average to fertile, humus rich, neutral to acidic** and **moist**. Leaves may scorch if the soil is not moist enough. This fern is an aggressive spreader that reproduces by spores. Unwanted plants can be pulled up and composted or given away.

## Tips

Ostrich fern appreciates a moist woodland garden and is often found growing wild alongside woodland streams and creeks. Useful in shaded borders, this plant is quick to spread, to the delight of those who enjoy the young fronds as a culinary delicacy.

## Recommended

*M. struthiopteris* (*M. pennsylvanica*) forms a circular cluster of slightly arching, feathery fronds. Stiff, brown, fertile fronds, covered in reproductive spores, stick up in the centre of the cluster in late summer and persist through winter. These are popular for dried flower arrangements.

**Also called:** fiddlehead fern
**Features:** perennial fern; foliage; habit
**Height:** 90 cm–1.5 m (3–5')
**Spread:** 12–90 cm (5–36") or more
**Hardiness:** zones 1–8

# Reed Grass
## *Calamagrostis*

*C. x acutiflora* 'Karl Foerster'

This is a graceful, metamorphic grass that changes its habit and flower colour throughout the seasons. The slightest breeze keeps this grass in perpetual motion.

## Growing

Reed grass grows best in **full sun**. The soil should be **fertile, moist** and **well drained**. Heavy clay and dry soils are tolerated. It may be susceptible to rust in cool, wet summers or in areas with poor air circulation. Rain and heavy snow may cause it to flop temporarily, but it quickly bounces back. Cut back to 5–10 cm (2–4") in very early spring before growth begins. Divide when it begins to die out in the centre.

## Tips

Whether it's used as a single, stately focal point, in small groupings or in large drifts, this is a desirable, low-maintenance grass. It combines well with perennials that bloom in late summer and fall.

## Recommended

*C.* **x** *acutiflora* **'Karl Foerster'** (Foerster's feather reed grass), the most popular selection, forms a loose mound of green foliage from which the airy bottlebrush flowers emerge in June. The flowering stems have a loose, arching habit when they first emerge but grow more stiff and upright over the summer. Other cultivars include **'Overdam,'** a compact, less hardy selection with white leaf edges.

**Features:** open habit becomes upright; silvery pink flowers turn rich tan; green foliage turns bright gold in fall; winter interest
**Height:** 90 cm–1.5 m (3–5')
**Spread:** 60–90 cm (24–36")
**Hardiness:** zones 4–8

*If you like how reed grass holds its flowers high above its mounded foliage, consider* Deschampsia *(tufted hair grass) and* Molinia *(moor grass) and their species and cultivars.*

# Ribbon Grass

*Phalaris*

P. arundinacea 'Picta' (above)
P. arundinacea 'Strawberries & Cream' (below)

*Because ribbon grass is so tolerant of wet soil, it is often included in the marginal plantings of ponds. In a container it can be grown in up to 30 cm (12") of water.*

This brightly striped grass forms large, attractive clumps that provide shelter to any small wildlife that visits or shares your garden.

### Growing

Ribbon grass grows well in **full sun to partial shade**. The soil should be of **average fertility** and **moist**. Even wet soils are tolerated. It is best to plant ribbon grass in large, sunken containers to control its spread. When it outgrows its container, divide ribbon grass in spring or early summer. The previous year's growth should be cut back in spring.

### Tips

Ribbon grass is ideal for damp areas of the garden where plants less tolerant of moisture tend to rot. It also does well in mixed container plantings and is a good choice for beds with solid borders, such as driveways and sidewalks, that can restrict its spread. In beds and borders it should be planted in sunken containers so it doesn't overwhelm less vigorous companions.

### Recommended

**P. arundinacea** forms quick-spreading clumps of long, narrow, sometimes yellow-striped leaves. Cultivars with brightly striped foliage, in colours such as pink, cream and green, have been developed.

**Features:** evergreen, perennial grass; winter interest; shelters wildlife
**Height:** 60 cm–1.5 m (2–5')
**Spread:** 90 cm (36") to indefinite
**Hardiness:** zones 2–8

# Sensitive Fern
*Onoclea*

*O. sensibilis* (above & below)

A common sight along stream banks and in wooded areas, these native ferns thrive in moist and shaded conditions.

## Growing

Sensitive ferns grow best in **light shade** but tolerate full shade and partial shade. The fronds can scorch if exposed to too much sun. The soil should be **fertile, humus rich** and **moist**. Some drought is tolerated. These plants are sensitive to frost and can be easily damaged by late and early frosts.

## Tips

Sensitive ferns like to live in damp, shady places. Include them in shaded borders, woodland gardens and other locations with protection from the wind.

## Recommended

*O. sensibilis* forms a mass of light green, deeply lobed, arching fronds. Fertile fronds are produced in late summer and persist through winter. The spores are produced in structures that look like black beads, which give the fertile fronds a decorative appearance that makes them a popular addition to floral arrangements.

*Strangely enough, this species is native to both eastern North America and eastern Asia—two places a world apart from one another.*

**Features:** deciduous, perennial fern; attractive foliage **Height:** 60 cm (24") **Spread:** indefinite **Hardiness:** zones 4–8

# Switch Grass
## *Panicum*

*P. virgatum* cultivar (above)
*P. virgatum* 'Heavy Metal' (below)

*Switch grass' delicate, airy panicles fill gaps in the garden border and can be cut for fresh or dried arrangements.*

Native to the prairie grasslands, switch grass naturalizes equally well in an informal border and a natural meadow.

### Growing
Switch grass thrives in **full sun, light shade** and **partial shade**. The soil should be of **average fertility** and **well drained**, but both moist and dry soils and conditions ranging from heavy clay to lighter sandy soil are tolerated.

Cut it back to 5–10 cm (2–4") from the ground in early spring. The flower stems may break under heavy, wet snow or in exposed, windy sites.

### Tips
Plant switch grass singly in small gardens, in large groups in spacious borders or at the edges of ponds or pools for a dramatic, whimsical effect. The seed heads attract birds and the foliage changes colour in fall, so place this plant where you can enjoy both features.

### Recommended
**P. virgatum** (switch grass) is suited to wild meadow gardens. Some of its popular cultivars include **'Heavy Metal'** (blue switch grass), an upright plant with narrow, steely blue foliage flushed with gold and burgundy in fall; and **'Prairie Sky'** (blue switch grass), an arching plant with deep blue foliage.

**Features:** clumping habit; green, blue or burgundy foliage; airy panicles of flowers; fall colour; winter interest
**Height:** 90 cm–1.5 m (3–5')
**Spread:** 75–90 cm (30–36")
**Hardiness:** zones 3–8

# Glossary

**Acidic soil:** soil with a pH lower than 7.0

**Annual:** a plant that germinates, flowers, sets seed and dies in one growing season

**Alkaline soil:** soil with a pH higher than 7.0

**Basal foliage:** leaves that form from the crown, at the base of the plant

**Bract:** a modified leaf at the base of a flower or flower cluster

**Corm:** a bulb-like, food-storing, underground stem, resembling a bulb without scales

**Crown:** the part of the plant at or just below soil level where the shoots join the roots

**Cultivar:** a cultivated plant variety with one or more distinct differences from the species, e.g., in flower colour or disease resistance

**Deadhead:** to remove spent flowers to maintain a neat appearance and encourage a longer blooming season

**Direct sow:** to sow seeds directly in the garden

**Dormancy:** a period of plant inactivity, usually during winter or unfavourable conditions

**Double flower:** a flower with an unusually large number of petals

**Espalier:** a tree trained from a young age to grow on a single plane—often along a wall or fence

**Genus:** a category of biological classification between the species and family levels; the first word in a scientific name indicates the genus

**Grafting:** a type of propagation in which a stem or bud of one plant is joined onto the rootstock of another plant of a closely related species

**Hardy:** capable of surviving unfavourable conditions, such as cold weather or frost, without protection

**Hip:** the fruit of a rose, containing the seeds

**Humus:** decomposed or decomposing organic material in the soil

**Hybrid:** a plant resulting from natural or human-induced cross-breeding between varieties, species or genera

**Neutral soil:** soil with a pH of 7.0

**Offset:** a horizontal branch that forms at the base of a plant and produces new plants from buds at its tips

**Panicle:** a compound flower structure with groups of flowers on short stalks

**Perennial:** a plant that takes three or more years to complete its life cycle

**pH:** a measure of acidity or alkalinity; the soil pH influences availability of nutrients for plants

**Rhizome:** a root-like, food-storing stem that grows horizontally at or just below soil level, from which new shoots may emerge

**Rootball:** the root mass and surrounding soil of a plant

**Seedhead:** dried, inedible fruit that contains seeds; the fruiting stage of the inflourescence

**Self-seeding:** reproducing by means of seeds without human assistance, so that new plants constantly replace those that die

**Semi-double flower:** a flower with petals in two or three rings

**Single flower:** a flower with a single ring of typically four or five petals

**Species:** the fundamental unit of biological classification; the entity from which cultivars and varieties are derived

**Standard:** a shrub or small tree grown with an erect main stem, accomplished either through pruning and training or by grafting the plant onto a tall, straight stock

**Sucker:** a shoot that comes up from the root, often some distance from the plant; it can be separated to form a new plant once it develops its own roots

**Tender:** incapable of surviving the climatic conditions of a given region and requiring protection from frost or cold

**Tuber:** the thick section of a rhizome bearing nodes and buds

**Variegation:** foliage that has more than one colour, often patched or striped or bearing leaf margins of a different colour

**Variety:** a naturally occurring variant of a species

# Index of Recommended Plant Names

Main entries are in **boldface**; botanical names are in *italics*.

# Author Biographies

**Duncan Kelbaugh** is known to many New Brunswick gardeners from his regular appearances on Rogers Television's "First Local," as garden columnist for the *Saint John Telegraph Journal* and as frequent respondent to CBC's "Good Questions." Duncan is a certified horticultural technician with a B.Sc. in Forestry and has owned and operated Brunswick Nurseries for the past 30 years. He and co-author Alison Beck also collaborated on *Gardening Month by Month in the Maritimes*.

**Alison Beck** is a professional garden writer who has been gardening since she was a child. Author of over two dozen books on gardening, her writing showcases her talent for practical advice and her passion for gardening. Alison has a diploma in Horticultural Technology as well as a degree in Creative Writing from York University.

# Acknowledgements

Thanks to fellow gardeners Judy Whalen and Peter Kinsella, and to horticulturist Jim Landry for help in preparing this text. — *Duncan Kelbaugh*